Investing in Collectables

Investing in Collectables

An Investor's Guide to Turning
Your Passion into a Portfolio

CHARLES BEELAERTS
WITH KEVIN FORDE

Wrightbooks

First published 2011 by Wrightbooks
an imprint of John Wiley & Sons Australia, Ltd
42 McDougall Street, Milton Qld 4064

Office also in Melbourne

Typeset in 11.5/14 pt Garamond

© Charles Beelaerts and Kevin Forde 2011

The moral rights of the authors have been asserted

National Library of Australia Cataloguing-in-Publication data:

Author:	Beelaerts, Charles.
Title:	Investing in Collectables / Charles Beelaerts; contributor, Kevin Forde.
ISBN:	9781742468198 (pbk.)
Notes:	Includes index.
Subjects:	Collectors and collecting. Investments. Collectibles.
Other Authors/Contributors:	Forde, Kevin.
Dewey Number:	790.132

Cover images: library and books © Yellowj, 2010. Used under license from Shutterstock.com; framed painting © Sandra Cunningham, 2010. Used under license from Shutterstock.com; wine bottle © GorillaAttack, 2010. Used under license from Shutterstock.com; Victorian coin © Scott Latham, 2010. Used under license from Shutterstock.com; fob watch © iStockphoto.com/Angelo Marcantonio.

Printed in China by Printplus Limited

10 9 8 7 6 5 4 3 2 1

Disclaimer
The material in this publication is of the nature of general comment only, and does not represent professional advice. It is not intended to provide specific guidance for particular circumstances and it should not be relied on as the basis for any decision to take action or not take action on any matter which it covers. Readers should obtain professional advice where appropriate, before making any such decision. To the maximum extent permitted by law, the authors and publisher disclaim all responsibility and liability to any person, arising directly or indirectly from any person taking or not taking action based upon the information in this publication.

Contents

About the authors

Charles Beelaerts is an economics graduate of the University of Sydney and a graduate of Harvard Business School. He is a financial consultant and author who has previously worked as an analyst for banks and investment firms.

Kevin Forde holds a Master of Economics degree from the University of NSW, where he has lectured for 10 years. He has worked as an industrial analyst and as a funds manager.

Acknowledgements

The input of Anne Cummins of Sydney Artefacts Conservation in chapter 4 and in other parts of the book is gratefully acknowledged. Thanks are also due to Ian Westbrook of Westbrook Financial Communications for his help with the 'fascinating collectables'. Finally, a special thank you to the team at John Wiley & Sons for their work on the book.

Introduction

This book is about investing in collectables. There are no hard and fast rules about what is collectable and the range can vary from such things as lucky charms worth virtually nothing to Old Masters worth millions. However, the focus of this book is how to make a profit out of collecting and this excludes many items that you can legitimately claim as 'collectables' — as they have no real value to other people. One area that is specifically excluded is mass-produced items because one of the features of a profitable collectable market is limited supply. As you might expect, the fewer there is of a collectable in existence, the more valuable it is.

Potential returns

There is worldwide evidence suggesting that investors are turning to collectables to provide better returns than share and fixed interest markets. For example, the current Capgemini and Merrill Lynch World Wealth Report found that investors were seeking items that are perceived to have tangible long-term value. The two categories that the report found most in demand were art and 'other collectables', such as coins, antiques and wine. Auction houses have also recently reported increased demand for these items. For example, according to Artprice, global fine art auctions raised US$3.8 billion in six months, which was nearly as much as for the whole of the previous year. While the amount raised is not high in absolute terms—the turnover of Woodside Petroleum on the Australian Securities Exchange on one day alone can exceed A$4 billion—it represents a significant upwards trend. Note that Artprice's figure is for fine art auctions only and it does not include private and dealer sales.

Did you know ... Collectables do not correlate strongly with other investments such as shares, bonds or property. In bad economic times collectables often hold their value.

Similarly investment returns are good. The Mei Moses All Art Index, which tracks auction prices, increased by 13.5 per cent in six months compared with a fall of 6.5 per cent in the S&P 500 Index. The Liv-ex Fine Wine Investables Index, which tracks the price of fine wines from 24 chateaux in Bordeaux, increased by 27.2 per cent in eight months. Table 1 shows the adjusted annual return to investors who invested in these indices.

Table 1: comparison returns

	Mei Moses All Art Index	Liv-ex Fine Wine Investables Index	S&P 500 Index
Time period of index	6 months to 30 June 2010	8 months to 31 August 2010	6 months to 30 June 2010
Increase over period	13.5%	27.2%	–06.5%
Annualised return	27.0% p.a.	40.8% p.a.	–13.0% p.a.

Source: adapted from the *Wall Street Journal*.

Note that in table 1 commissions are ignored but they are much higher with art and wine than they are with shares.

Given the vast range of items that people collect it is not possible to generalise about the investment potential of collectables—just as some investment properties can increase in value while others are falling. But if you put the time and effort into identifying desirable collectables—just as you would in identifying 'growth shares' on the sharemarket—it is certainly possible to make handsome profits.

Why invest in collectables?

Apart from above average returns potential, there are other reasons for investing in collectables. These include the following:

- Since collectables are tangible assets where supply may be restricted, they provide an excellent hedge against inflation. If inflation is running at 3 per cent per annum, you need at least this rate of return to keep pace and collectables generally provide this. When financial markets are uncertain there are benefits in owning tangible assets.

- Collectables do not correlate strongly with other investments, such as shares, bonds or property. In bad economic times collectables often hold their value.

- Collectables do not exhibit the same level of volatility found, for example, in the sharemarket. Collectables do not usually increase markedly in price one day and fall back the next, although they are not traded in the same way.

- An investor in collectables does not need to monitor their performance as often as investors in other assets. You can 'buy and forget' to a greater extent than you can with many other types of investments.

- But like any other investment, collectables can rise and fall in price and they can certainly lose considerable value if they go out of fashion. So as an investor in collectables, you need to make decisions with your head, not your heart.

- If all else fails, a collector has invested in items that they can enjoy and that enhance their lifestyle.

Investment collecting is a long-term venture. Most collectables need to be kept for five to 10 years to show good appreciation in value.

In addition you can begin operating as an investment collector in a small way. For example, you can buy an ancient Roman coin for a few hundred dollars or a piece of antique furniture for the same price. You can also buy a good painting for only $1000. To buy an investment property costs hundreds of thousands of dollars or a share portfolio will cost you a minimum of $5000.

Table 2 (on pages xvi–xvii) reveals the main features of investing in collectables compared with shares, fixed interest securities and investment property.

Arguments against collectables as an investment

The chief arguments against investing in collectables are that it requires a high degree of skill and that buying and selling commissions are high and are calculated as a percentage of the price of the collectable. Consequently, it is essential to calculate your investment return after tax and after commissions. Also, there are storage and insurance costs that have to be factored in and collectables usually produce no income to offset these expenses, and you generally cannot negatively gear collectables. Consequently, critics say that shares and property are better investments.

Not everyone thinks that collectables are good investments, but those who don't think so tend not to be investment collectors themselves. You need to catch the bug first.

These issues are addressed in later chapters, but at this stage it needs to be said that you must have a genuine interest in collectables to be a successful investment collector. It is true that profitably investing in collectables requires a degree of skill that you cannot hope to acquire if you do not enjoy researching and learning about your speciality. This is just the first step as you have to buy and sell well, too. It is also true that collectables usually do not generate an income stream and you may have to wait for years to get a return. However, during this time you derive the benefits of owning the collectables, including the enjoyment of their aesthetic appeal, which is generally missing with other forms of investment.

This book is written for genuine investment collectors. If you have $5000 to invest, and any investment will do as long as it provides a high return, you will also benefit from reading our earlier book *Understanding Investments: An Australian Investor's Guide to Stock Market, Property and Cash-Based Investments, 5th Edition* (Wrightbooks, 2010).

Potential for capital gain

Except for art rentals—a highly specialised area—the return from investing in collectables is made up wholly of capital appreciation. As an appropriate investment time horizon for collectables is five to 10 years, it represents a long period during which you receive no income. At the end of this time horizon you might incur a loss as prices can fall as well as increase. This emphasises why you need to invest in something that you like. It also emphasises just how important it is to make a good decision when you invest in a collectable. To do this you need to have become an 'amateur expert' in your field, which requires extensive research before you make your first purchase. There is simply no substitute for doing the work that this entails. Good investment collectors are not lazy by nature, although once you have made a purchase you can relax somewhat.

It should also be noted that in a low interest rate environment the 'opportunity cost' of investing in collectables for capital appreciation is minimal. The opportunity cost of an investment is what you give up by not investing the same amount of money in an alternative project. For example, if you have $5000 to invest and you can get 6 per cent per annum from an online savings account, you are only foregoing $300 a year by investing in collectables. Compare this with a situation where you could get 20 per cent per annum when you would be foregoing $1000 a year.

Table 2: collectables as an investment

Criterion	Shares	Fixed interest	Investment property	Collectables
Aesthetic value	Nil	Nil	Some	High
Buying and selling costs	Very low	Very Low	Moderate	Extremely variable but can be very high
Income generated	Regular dividends on many shares	Regular interest payments	Rental income	None except for rentals
Potential for capital gains	Good with some shares	Possible if interest rates fall	Good	Generally good, but highly variable
Markets where traded	National and international. Uniform prices.	National and international. Uniform prices.	Regional. Prices vary markedly between different locations.	Market specific. No markets in some areas. High cost when accessing international markets.
Ease of buying and selling	Money received in 3 days	Money received in 3 days	Variable. Buying and selling can take several months.	Complicated as markets may be difficult to access. Multiple avenues to consider.

Criterion	Shares	Fixed interest	Investment property	Collectables
Potential for negative gearing	Good	None	Very good	Only possible with rentals
Capital gains tax liability	Payable on any capital gain	Payable on any capital gain	Payable on any capital gain	Payable on collectables that cost more than $500. Cars costing $10000 or less are excluded.
Ongoing maintenance	None	None	Repairs and renovations as needed	Can be very high. Repairs should be avoided. Storage important.
Insurance	Not needed	Not needed	Includes property insurance and mortgage repayment insurance	Depends on collectables. Some covered by household contents insurance. Special cover may be needed.
Availability of information	Very good	Very good	Good	Research necessary. Much needed information costs money. Time-consuming. Often difficult to know how much a collectable will sell for.
Investment time horizon	Short, medium and long-term	Short, medium and long-term	Medium to long-term	Except for speculation, long-term

Liquidity

Shares and bonds are very liquid investments because you can generally sell them and receive payment in three business days. Property is less liquid because it may take months to sell. Collectables are the least liquid of all, but this can be an advantage because it can lead to the avoidance of poor short-term market-driven investment decisions. On the other hand, the market may move against you while you are waiting to sell.

Collectables as an asset class

There are four prime asset classes, namely, shares (domestic and international), fixed-interest securities (domestic and international), property and cash. From time to time, promoters of investments will attempt to enhance the credibility of their investments by encouraging the investing public to consider them as an asset class in their own right. In previous years, gold has been suggested as a separate asset class, while in 2001 there was an attempt to classify hedge funds as 'alternative' investments. The truth is that neither are separate asset classes. Nevertheless, the *Australian Financial Review* in October 2008 described art as an 'asset class for all kinds of weather'.

In this book

Chapter 1 examines the advantages and disadvantages of collectables from an investment viewpoint and reveals the key determinants of value. In chapter 2 we review several types of collectables, including art, wine, stamps, coins, banknotes, books, memorabilia, and fads, hobbies and obsessions. Chapter 3 covers international markets. Conservation, restoration and insurance are dealt with in chapter 4, while tax and other legislation are considered in chapter 5. Chapter 6 discusses buying and selling privately and through dealers. Chapter 7 looks at buying and selling at auction, and chapter 8 examines buying and selling online. Chapter 9 looks at 'dos and don'ts' when buying and selling collectables, chapter 10 examines fraud, and chapter 11 reviews how to make money from investing in collectables. The 'Useful resources' section then provides details for sources of further information.

Fascinating collectables ...

Classic wallpaper

Over the last 100 years the popularity of wallpaper has been subjected to boom and bust. From 1960 to about 1980 it was very popular in homes, but then householders demonstrated a distinct preference for painted or untreated surfaces and the industry collapsed. In recent times wallpaper has made a comeback and the same wallpaper that was worth only a few dollars a roll back in the 1980s is now worth hundreds of dollars a roll. However, not all wallpaper is considered 'classic' and therefore valuable, even if it is 50 years old or more. Only about 1 per cent of the wallpaper produced is in this category. Hence, the main task is to determine exactly what is collectable. People who bought large quantities of classic wallpaper when it went out of favour in the late 1980s are now sitting on sizeable investments. The main risk, of course, is that the demand for wallpaper will again collapse as tastes change.

Classic designs that are collectable nowadays include fanciful designs of the 1950s, which sell for $50 a roll, and psychedelic patterns of the late 1960s, which sell for about $100 a roll. However, probably the most well-known name in Australian wallpaper is designer Florence Broadhurst, who produced more than 800 designs before she was murdered in an unsolved crime in 1977. A stained-glass pattern of Broadhurst's that was produced for an interior designer in Sydney in the late 1960s is worth about $200 a roll. A 1959 Florence Broadhurst sample book has an estimated value of $1000 and it is estimated that six to seven matching rolls of hers would be worth about $1000.

Collectables as an investment

Buying art, antiques and other collectables with the aim of making a profit is like no other form of investing. With shares, bonds, investment property, derivatives, hedge funds and other more mainstream investments it is essential that you do not develop a love and passion for the area in which you are investing. Some shareholders make the mistake of falling in love with their shares, which distorts their judgement when making decisions about buying and selling them. With collectables generally the opposite is true; you need to be interested in, and have an appreciation for, the items you collect. Otherwise you will lack the eye for detail and expertise of the true collector. It is also essential that your particular collectables appeal to you because you may own them for many years. In some cases your passion may lead you to collect objects which do not appreciate in value; for example, Coca-Cola cans or key rings. Clearly, here the enjoyment factor is important as the potential for profit is limited.

There is a wide range of collectables in which you could invest. Depending on what is in favour, they include the following:

- 19th-century Australian colonial and traditional painting
- Australian impressionists
- indigenous art
- modern Australian painting
- contemporary Australian art
- original prints
- British art
- Chinese ceramics and works of art
- Japanese art
- Art Nouveau and Art Deco ceramics, glass, furniture and works of art
- silver
- Australian jewels
- Australian glass
- English, German and Italian glass
- antiquities
- Islamic works of art, including rugs and pottery
- Australian colonial furniture
- English and European furniture
- English and European pottery and porcelain
- wine
- coins and medals
- stamps
- books
- cars/automobilia
- music and sport memorabilia.

Collectables including stamps, wine, paintings, coins, furniture, jewellery, rare books, sporting and music memorabilia, glassware and china are generally considered to be investments for the long-term. Collecting and buying and selling them for profit requires special skill and expertise to assess their authenticity, value, condition, rarity and general potential for appreciation. If you have an eye on profit when selecting an area of collectables in which to invest, focus on those that appeal to dealers and auction houses because this helps to ensure fairness and liquidity.

In 1974 the British Rail Pension Fund (Railpen) decided to invest in collectables as a hedge against inflation. As a result it invested a total of UK£40 million in over 2400 works of art. The artworks included paintings and sculptures, and many were lent to museums to reduce storage and insurance costs. In the early 1980s index-linked government bonds were introduced, which represented a hedge against inflation. Consequently Railpen decided to sell its portfolio of artwork. The final sales of artwork took place in late 2003 and by then Railpen had realised UK£172 million for a profit of UK£132 million over a period of approximately 30 years. This amounted to a return of 4 per cent better than the rate of inflation over this 30-year period.

Often the skills required to make money in a specialist area are developed over a long period of interest in the collectable. To acquire the necessary skills there are many information resources available, ranging from books, magazines, the internet, and television and radio programs through to attending auctions and exhibitions, trade fairs and antique shows, or visiting dealers and seeking the opinion of experts. While you can always refer to external sources or the specialist opinion of others, you will still need to develop your own understanding of your speciality area to know what to look for and which questions to ask.

Did you know ... An 1813 NSW Colonial Dump coin in extremely fine condition was worth only $165 in 1967. In December 2008 it was worth $210000. An extremely fine Holey Dollar, out of which the Dump was made, is today worth around $330000.

Advantages and disadvantages of collectables as an investment

For some people the disadvantages of investing in collectables outweigh the advantages, while for others it is the enjoyment they receive from collecting that swings their preferences in favour of collectables investing. Whether you decide to invest in collectables rather than traditional asset classes comes down to how comfortable you are with this form of investing—and how much time you want to spend on researching particular collectables. Perhaps the overriding consideration is that you choose an area in which you are personally interested so that you derive nonfinancial benefits in the course of making a profit.

Advantages of collectables as an investment

There are advantages and disadvantages associated with investing in collectables with the aim of making a profit. Advantages include:

- As collectables are generally a long-term investment you can buy them and store them securely and just forget about them. Unlike more conventional investments, such as shares or property, you don't have to monitor their progress daily or monthly. Unrealised capital gains are not taxed. Hence you can buy collectables that appreciate in value and manage your tax liability by not selling them.

- Although collectables go in and out of fashion, they are usually not as volatile as traditional investments. Collectables tend not to be positively correlated with movements in the traditional asset classes. For example, when the sharemarket or the property market is trending downwards, collectables tend to hold their value or even increase. During the global financial crisis when world sharemarkets fell 30 to 40 per cent, the value of gold increased. Collectables that contained a high proportion of gold, such as some jewellery and gold coins, increased in value as well.

- Unless you are in business as a collector, or you are in the business of renting out your collectables, you do not pay income tax on your profits (see chapter 5). Investing in collectables is a hobby that can pay off.

- The markets for collectables are much less regulated than financial markets. This means that your potential for making money is less determined by government economic policies and more determined by supply and demand.

- The apparent lack of liquidity with collectables can mean that you are less prone to making poor short-term market-driven investment decisions when you are tempted to sell.

- A collection of coins, stamps, books, art, glassware or other items may have a value as a collection that exceeds the value of the sum of its parts, which allows more affordable access to the collectable and greater gain when the set is complete.

- A low interest rate regime means that there is less of an income penalty for you if you choose to put money in collectables. This means that because the prevailing rate of interest is low — and next to nothing in some overseas countries — the income you forego by not investing at these rates is also low. What you give up in interest on a bank deposit is much less significant than if interest rates were much higher.

- In testing economic times and on occasions when the sharemarket is under severe stress, investors in collectables feel less pressure to hurry a sale simply because the climate has changed for the worse.

Did you know ... One of the main attractions of diamonds is that they are an excellent store of portable wealth. For example, 40 high-quality 1-carat diamonds worth US$1 million can be housed in a container the size of a small paperback book.

Disadvantages of collectables as an investment

There are several disadvantages that you need to be aware of when you are investing in collectables. Disadvantages include:

- The transaction costs associated with buying and selling collectables can be significantly higher than those associated with other forms of investing. Depending on what you buy and how you buy it, you may be liable for a commission of 10 per cent or more on both the buying and selling price. This compares with buying and selling shares, where commissions can be as low as 0.15 per cent, and when selling property, where agents' commissions are around 2 per cent.

- There may be additional costs associated with security, insurance and caring for your collectables. While an investment property carries with it similar charges, there are no such costs attached to investing in shares and bonds.

- Collectables are often illiquid investments and you may be unable to get your money back when you want to, even at a reduced price. It is true that a property may take months to sell, but depending on the collectable it may take years to find a buyer. On the other hand, shares and bonds can always be sold on financial markets and you receive your money within days.

- The markets for collectables are fragmented, whereas the markets for shares and bonds are uniform across territories. If you are selling shares or bonds, you are quoted the same market price no matter where you live. Collectables are more saleable in some locations than others; for example, paintings and antiques are usually limited to sales in capital cities if you want the best price.

- When you own collectables there is usually no freely available up-to-date measure of value for them. You have to research to find out current prices or recently obtained prices, but even then you never know a collectable's conclusive market price until you sell it. It is not until the time of sale that a price is set; before this all you can obtain is an approximate value. Conversely, when buying a collectable, you can review sellers' prices and conduct research, but you will never know if you have paid too much for an item. In contrast, when buying and selling shares and bonds, the prices are quoted daily—and indeed every minute on trading days.

- Except for art rentals, you do not derive an income stream from collectables. There is in effect an annual opportunity cost equal to what you could earn from the best alternative investment.

For example, say you could earn 6 per cent per annum from investing in an online savings account. If you invest $10 000 in a painting, you would be foregoing $600 before tax per year in income. Your painting would need to rise in value by at least that much in the first year for you to be equally well off.

- There is always the possibility that a collectable will become damaged. A small chip on a piece of porcelain could significantly reduce its value, as could a scratch on an otherwise valuable coin.

- If you invest in collectables as a hobby, you cannot claim the interest on borrowings you make to purchase a collectable as a tax deduction. Furthermore you cannot add interest expenses to the cost base of a collectable, so it does not reduce your capital gains tax liability (see chapter 5). In contrast, you can 'negatively gear' investments in shares and property.

Did you know …

Invitations to attend the opening of Australia's first Parliament on 9 May 1901 in Melbourne are sought after by collectors. The value varies depending on who was invited but $1000 for each invitation may be taken as a guide.

Special features of collectable markets

Collectables are a unique kind of investment, which means that individual markets will behave in uncertain and unpredictable ways. No two types of collectables are the same and different factors will affect their values at any one time and over time. For example, modern artworks will differ from each other with regard to such things as artist, genre, era, condition, rarity and size, and each painting has to be assessed individually. In addition, modern artwork as a collectable category has different characteristics from other collectables. In determining what is good to invest in you need to be sensitive to these nuances and develop a feel for the features of your collectables that render them valuable.

Variable appreciation rates

Many novice collectable investors seem to assume that the value of their collectables will appreciate over time. This is frequently the case, but sometimes it isn't and you can end up with a lot of worthless junk. For example, Victorian furniture was once very popular and buying and selling pieces led to handsome profits. In today's market it is out of fashion and collectors who purchased pieces at high prices have seen their holdings fall in value when selling.

The rate of increase in the values of collectables will vary between different collectables and also over time. An important factor you have to consider is supply and demand. Demand can be defined as the number of serious buyers for an item and supply can be defined as the actual number of items in existence. Obviously, the more buyers there are and the rarer the item, the higher the price will be (other things being equal).

Market proximity

When considering supply and demand you also have to take into account market proximity. If you are in Australia holding a rare Roman coin and most of the buyers for your coin are overseas, you will probably be better off selling the coin overseas. The alternative is that the buyers come to you, which will limit the potential market for the coin. When deciding what you want to collect you need to consider the collectables' international as well as local appeal.

Market fluctuation

In general, when the sharemarket is rising most share prices are also increasing. But with collectables you can find that there can be strong demand in one sector of the market—for example, indigenous art—while other collectable markets are languishing. Consequently, you need to carefully consider the type of collectables you own or in which you are considering investing. Specific types of collectables, such as a significant painting or a rare book, will tend to increase in value more quickly than more widely held collectables, such as wine, coins, stamps and comic books.

Limited liquidity

Unless you choose to collect something that is out of the realm of mainstream collectables, make sure you establish that a liquid market exists for your area of specialisation—that is, a market where there are usually numerous buyers and sellers. Otherwise you will encounter serious problems if you need to sell quickly. You may not buy with the intention of selling quickly afterwards, but unforeseen circumstances may compel you to dispose of your purchases before you otherwise would. If collecting for you is a novelty, it is not so important because you are unlikely to be in it for the money.

Income stream generation

If an income stream is important to you, build a collection of a large number of relatively inexpensive collectables so that you can sell off some items when you want money. If you only have a few valuable items in your collection, you cannot do this. For example, if you have $10 000 to invest and you buy only one item, you cannot sell a part of it if you want a few thousand dollars. You would have to sell the item. On the other hand, if you buy five items of $2000 each and you need a few thousand dollars, you can sell one or two items and still have the remainder.

Developing your investment strategy

As with any investment you need a strategic plan—otherwise you will end up with an investment portfolio that is unbalanced and with no overall coherent strategy. Without a strategy you can easily find yourself buying items because they are available rather than because they fit into your overall collection.

Developing an investment strategy requires that you address a range of issues, including your areas of interest, your investment goals, your investment time horizon, your financial resources and your attitude to risk. Potentially there are a large number of collectables in which you can invest and you need to adapt your investment strategy to your chosen field. The following concentrates on relevant issues that will help you formulate an investment strategy.

Fascinating collectables ...

Trans-Australia Airlines memorabilia

Trans-Australia Airlines (TAA), which became Australian Airlines in 1986 and which was merged with Qantas in 1993, has its own museum in Melbourne, the TAA Museum, <www.taamuseum.org.au>. TAA had its first flight in 1946 from Melbourne to Sydney and it was the first airline in Australia to serve a hot meal on a domestic flight. In 1960 it was also the first commercial airline in the world to be subjected to an attempted hijacking. Today copies of newspapers covering the story are worth about $25. There is also the TAA 25 Year Club, which comprises people who served 25 years or more with the airline and which has been instrumental in maintaining the TAA Museum. Today the museum has more than 150000 items in its collection.

There is a lively secondary market in TAA memorabilia. Young passengers were given a Junior Flyers Badge when they flew with TAA and these sell at auction for $40 to $70 depending on age and condition. More valuable are the badges given to junior frequent flyers, but these are very rare and hard to find. Known as the 50 Hours Badge these would sell for $100 or more, and as they cost nothing the return on investment is infinite. TAA posters are rare and valuable. They featured a model rather than a real-life TAA hostess and had the slogan 'Fly TAA. The Friendly Way'. One with a blue background from the early 1950s sold at auction in Melbourne for $5000. Earlier versions with a yellow background are rarer and more valuable, but TAA enthusiasts have never seen one sold publicly.

Risk

An investment strategy should formally assess the risks you are taking. In doing this you will need to have regard for the price histories of different collectables. You will also have to confront the possibility of significant loss from your investing activities. As with any profit-making venture, you should not invest more than you can afford to lose.

In developing an investment strategy that accommodates risk you should consider diversifying your collectables portfolio. For example, you might choose to invest in contemporary Australian painting but it would be most unwise to put all your eggs in one basket. By having a spread of artists and time periods and genre, you limit your exposure to the one market. Alternatively you may opt for a balanced portfolio of collectables and buy some stamps and coins, some art, some furniture and antiques, and some jewellery. If one area performs badly, you have the other areas to fall back on. It is unlikely that all categories would fall in value simultaneously.

Availability of information

Initially you need to consider the availability of research information for your chosen field and its likely appeal to other collectors. You cannot make prudent investment decisions with a view to making a profit unless you know what to collect and the likely cost and the extent of the market. The first step in this process is to acquire knowledge and expertise.

Areas in which there are established markets are easier to research and values can be more readily assessed. It is also easier when it comes time to sell your collectables, which is especially important if you have to sell unexpectedly.

Quality verses quantity

You need to determine a strategy in terms of quality versus quantity. Higher quality items will increase in value more quickly, so it is better to spend a lot of money on one quality item than to buy many lesser quality items. You will have to wait longer to save enough money but this strategy will pay dividends in terms of capital appreciation. However, you have to balance this strategy against liquidity considerations. For example, if you indeed decide to go for quality over quantity and invest in just one or two higher priced items, you cannot sell a part of them if you need some money. You have to sell the complete item. On the other hand, if your purchases are directed at the art rental market, you will have to spend a minimum amount per item to be eligible. Only you can decide if your best strategy option is to collect a few high-priced items or many lower priced items.

Price histories taken from dealers and auctions provide you with a degree of comfort and a basis on which to assess prices of potential investments, the amount of capital required to acquire a range of investment grade items and a benchmark for determining quality.

Security and maintenance

You will need to take into account the likely security and maintenance requirements of the items you collect and whether you should insure them if you don't have adequate security. The condition of collectables is important both when you are considering buying them and when you are faced with maintaining them. Antiques lend themselves to being used in your home but if you collect them, make sure they are out of harm's way. Wine requires special storage arrangements, which can be expensive, while stamps and coins are easier to store. Vintage and classic cars require garaging, preferably away from salt air. You can hang paintings in your home and enjoy them while they hopefully appreciate in value, but it is wise to hang them away from sunlight.

Did you know ...

Australia's first gold coins were the Adelaide Assay Office A£1 pound coins. Uncirculated, these coins are now worth about $80 000 each.

Constraints on supply

Possibly the single most important factor in determining the value of a collectable is the number of items in existence. Generally speaking, the higher the number of items in existence, the lower their value. Scarcity or rarity can make a collectable valuable because when demand exceeds supply, a collectable's price will tend to rise. The age of an item is not in itself a determinant of value, except insofar as the older an item is the less likely it is that there will be many in existence. To decide on which area to specialise in you should focus on one where there is reputable documentary evidence available revealing the number of items in existence. This could be the number of coins or stamps minted, or the number of artworks by a particular artist, or the number of a specific model of classic car that has been made. Armed with documentary evidence you can assess the scarcity of different collectables that will underpin your choice of speciality.

Costs

The area you choose to specialise in will partly depend on your budget. It may not cost much to get started buying music memorabilia—for example, LP records—but a single painting could cost you many thousands of dollars. Similarly it costs little to start collecting first day covers, but a classic car could cost $50 000 or more. If you have a clear understanding of the amount you are able to spend, you will know what kind of collection you can build and you can aim to get the best value from your investment. For example, if you choose to invest in stamps which are part of a set, you could collect the individual stamps as your financial circumstances permit and then recoup an exponential gain when you sell the set as a whole

Your interests

Stick to what you are interested in as you cannot hope to become an expert in an area that has no appeal to you. You will soon lose interest and make poor buying and selling decisions. Unless you see yourself as a speculator, the time you spend improving your knowledge of an area will pay off because you will develop the skills necessary to assess true worth.

Investors of collectables generally prefer to have physical ownership of the assets rather than to own securities over companies that trade in the particular collectables or store the items long-term off site. You will derive more enjoyment and you're likely to make more money as there are fewer expenses involved with holding the collectable.

Time and cost preventing fraud

Consider how much time you will need to spend evaluating fakes and forgeries. Some collectables (for example, some sporting memorabilia) come with certificates of authenticity while others (for example, expensive antiques and paintings) have to be authenticated by an expert. Still others can be purchased directly from the source (for example, mint coins and banknotes), which circumvents the possibility of fraud. Potentially fraud can cost you a substantial amount of money. For example, in 2010 former US tennis star John McEnroe was sold two forged paintings for a total of US$2 million. The fraudster in this case was caught and he was found guilty of defrauding clients of US$120 million. He had to repay the money and he was also sent to prison In many other cases, however, the people responsible are not caught.

Your lifestyle

Focus on collecting items that are appropriate to your lifestyle. For example, it does not really make sense to collect Australian colonial furniture if you don't have the space to use it or if it doesn't fit with the decor of your modern apartment. If your collectables are to be kept at home and you have young children, there are some items that would be at risk, such as Italian glassware. Other problems may arise if you have pets. If your collectables are at risk of damage of breakage for these types of reasons, focus on areas of collecting where items can be kept in a safe place. For example, paintings high up on a wall are in a safe place while oriental rugs on the floor are not.

Did you know ... Antique rugs can fetch high prices. For example, a Ziegler & Company Persian rug circa 1890 sold in 2003 for US$21 600 even though it was faded with moth damage. Rugs such as this are best displayed and hung on walls.

Your time horizon

Your investment time horizon is a factor. Some collectables, such as jewellery, first day covers, wine and coins, may take many years to appreciate in value. Other areas, such as paintings and prints by well-known artists and indigenous art, can appreciate more quickly. So the area you choose to specialise in will partly be determined by how quickly you aim to make a profit, bearing in mind that there is no such thing as a guaranteed return. Many investors have found to their regret that the value of their collection depreciates rather than appreciates. For example, vintage art pottery is popular with some investment collectors but since excellent reproductions of the real thing are mass produced in China, this has depressed prices of original items and investment collectors have been burned. As another example of what can happen, an Australian bought an item of modern art while on vacation in the US for US$6000. He later went bankrupt and could only get $1000 for the painting. The value of collectables does not always increase, even if you hold onto them for a long period of time.

Speculation

Speculation is not confined to the sharemarket. A speculator in collectables may be defined as a person who has no love or passion for an object but seeks to buy and sell it with a view to making a fast profit. The pure focus on the monetary aspect is what distinguishes speculation from true investment collecting. Speculative collectors tend to 'jump on the bandwagon' when a category of collectables shows signs of taking off and take a quick profit if proved right. But because of the risk of being left with unfashionable collectables, speculation is not recommended for novice investors.

Carefully looked after, collectables are essentially permanent investments. It was never intended that they be the stimulus for speculation but opportunities nevertheless arise from time to time for savvy market players. Speculation is generally frowned upon by true collectors. However, as speculation heightens general market activity it is not looked upon disdainfully by all the participants in the markets for collectables. Although this book is not written for speculators, it is worth mentioning that there are some basic prerequisites to being a successful speculator. The first one is to have a detached view.

As with buying speculative stocks, it is common that speculators misinterpret markets at times and buy objects that do not in fact take off. You need to be able to differentiate between what is a quickly passing fad and what is sustainable to the extent that you can buy and sell before the collectables go out of fashion. You also have to be prepared to accept losses on some of the purchases you make. For example, some commercial businesses collect books that are out of print for resale to the public at high prices, with mark-ups of over 300 per cent not uncommon. However, sometimes these businesses are left with books that no-one ever wants, they have to pay for the storage and care of the item, and the sales that are actually made have to cover these losses.

It is often said when investing in shares that it is time in the market rather than timing the market that is important. It is generally the same when investing in collectables for profit. For example, when buying collectables it may be difficult to buy at the bottom of the market (particularly with antiques!), but the longer you hold them the greater the increase in capital appreciation you can generally expect to earn. The aim of successful speculation is to both buy and sell within a relatively short space of time. Speculators need to constantly monitor prices and markets to aid their timing in the market. They cannot 'buy and forget' to the same extent a conventional investment collector can, as a missed opportunity can have a significant impact on profits.

Speculators need to be more flexible than traditional investment collectors. The possibility always exists that what was once considered to be a passing fad can become permanent and you have to switch your thinking from quick profits to a longer-term view—or sell out and take a loss. This is not necessarily a bad thing, but you need to have the financial resources at your disposal to manage the change.

Finally, the more you buy and sell, as speculators do, the more likely it is that the Australian Taxation Office (ATO) will consider that you are conducting a business. As a result you will be liable to pay income tax on your profits (if any), although you will also be able to write off some of your costs as tax deductions.

Speculation is not for the faint-hearted. You may have many thousands of dollars tied up in collectables and be unaware how the markets will move. It is akin to gambling and as such carries high risks. Some collectables rise quickly to prominence only to fall as quickly a year or two later. Quick gains can occur but so can quick losses.

Did you know ... The influence of publicity in boosting demand for a particular collectable should not be underestimated. The more people who know about an item for sale, the greater the likelihood that prices will be pushed up. This can work against you when buying but it can work in your favour when selling.

Key points

- Collectables as an area of investment can be differentiated from mainstream investing in that you are seeking to derive satisfaction, enjoyment and profit.

- As with investing generally, to be successful in investing in collectables you will need to undertake extensive research, develop a consistent investment strategy and commit to an appropriate timeframe.

- There are numerous advantages and disadvantages associated with investing in collectables.

- A factor of fundamental importance in determining the value of collectables is supply and demand. Supply is the number of an item in existence and it may diminish over time. Demand can be defined as the number of serious buyers for an item.

- It is generally better to buy quality over quantity, unless you are deriving an income stream from your collection and you need liquidity.

- It is safer to buy collectables for which there are established markets — this provides better availability of information for both buyers and sellers, which is one of the major determiners in generating demand and realising profit.

- There are many areas of collectables in which you can specialise and when making your investment you should consider the availability of research information, maintenance requirements, the prevalence of fakes and forgeries, the costs of items, your investment time horizon and your lifestyle.

- Speculating is a special category of investment collecting that has its own rewards and pitfalls. It is a high risk activity and is not recommended for most investors.

2

Types of collectables

This chapter looks at a selection of collectables and evaluates their potential for generating a profit. Without knowing the personal circumstances of each reader it is not possible to know in advance whether an area of collectables is suitable or appropriate on the grounds of cost or other factors, such as storage or space considerations. Hence each type of collectable selected for review here has been assessed according to its investment potential solely in terms of its overall profitability. You are in the best position to know if a collectable fits your financial objectives.

Art

Like most collectables, art is the sort of investment you need to hold for five to 10 years. It is a buy-and-hold investment and not one where you should expect a quick profit. The art market is vast, so in theory there is a broad range of artworks from which to choose.

Generally speaking the market may be broken down into three categories:

- emerging artists
- mid-career artists
- established artists.

The first rule of thumb is not to overcommit yourself to any one artist—especially not in the emerging artist market. Buy just one piece and make sure it's a work you like because the reality is that it may not increase in value—and it may even drop in value. It is also essential to obtain a certificate of authenticity for an artwork, and this is especially true with emerging artists. The golden rule when purchasing any work of art is: do not buy anything that will not give you enjoyment when you display it in your own home.

Emerging artists

Emerging artists are those you most probably have never heard of, or who are at the beginnings of their careers. Their work can be obtained for a few thousand dollars or less. From an investment point of view, the chief advantage of these works of art is that there is considerable potential for capital appreciation if the artist comes into fashion. This is also an obvious disadvantage in that an emerging artist may never be widely appreciated, in which case there is little or no capital gain at all. Because of this, purchasing the artworks of emerging artists is akin to speculating and you have to expect high volatility of returns. You may make a good profit with an emerging artist, but even expert art advisers have difficulty predicting which emerging artists will actually make the big time. Therefore, if you invest in emerging artists, you are taking sizeable risks, so research carefully and don't overcommit yourself to one artist.

When investing in an emerging artist it is important that you find out something about the artist because generally little is publicly known about their work. For example, is the painting you are interested in part of a series? Does 'your' artwork possess anything unique to that series? Go for a large-scale piece, providing you have the space to show it, because it will stand out.

Works by emerging artists have the greatest scope for capital appreciation, but by the same token they may never take off. So only invest in them with funds earmarked for speculation. If you have less than $5000 to invest, you are generally going to be limited to emerging artists.

Mid-career artists

Mid-career artists are those artists who are actively creating a name for themselves. They may have established a reputation with art auction houses and have a history of winning prizes, and they may have attracted international interest. Compared with established artists, mid-career artists are also risky and the prices of their works can be volatile, but this also means there can be handsome profits to be made. Prices vary enormously but $5000 to $50 000 may be taken as a guide depending on the nature of the artwork.

When selecting a work by a mid-career artist choose an artist who is known to auction houses and galleries and who has won a prize or two, even if they are not well-known prizes. If you are faced with a dilemma of choosing one or two mid-career artists, or several emerging artists, or a combination of both, the general rule of thumb is that you should buy 'quality over quantity' so focus on the mid-career artists. Their works are also more suitable for renting out (see 'Art rentals' below).

Established artists

Established artists are often referred to as 'blue-chip' artists. They have confirmed a place in the art world and include local artists such as Sidney Nolan, Brett Whiteley and Arthur Boyd. Works by these artists may sell for hundreds of thousands or even millions of dollars. Although works by established artists are slower to appreciate, a pre-tax return of 10 per cent to 11 per cent per annum is typical, and this return is much less volatile than is the case with other categories of artists.

Art rentals

Providing you have a suitable work of art, there is an opportunity to derive rental income from it while you remain the owner. However, you need to select your artwork carefully and consult with an organisation that offers this facility before you make a purchase. In Australia the government and corporate sectors have displayed works of art in commercial buildings such as offices and hotels for many years and the recent trend is for organisations to rent rather than buy these artworks. The reason is that it involves less outlay and it enables businesses to change displays more often. The corporate rental market has created excellent opportunities for investors to buy portfolios of artwork that appeal to the corporate sector. Typical contracts run for two to three years and you can expect underwritten returns of 5 per cent to 8 per cent per annum.

A rental portfolio can be bought with self-managed super funds but you should talk to your financial adviser first.

Artworks suitable for rental start at approximately $10 000 to approximately $50 000. Artwork below this range is not appealing to corporations and other organisations, and above this range the rental premiums are too high. You will have to seek advice on which artwork is suitable for renting because not all artworks sold are appropriate. If you buy an artwork for rental, you will be obliged to pay additional costs over and above the purchase price as follows:

- Portfolio management fee to cover storage, transportation and insurance. This costs about $50 per work per year.

- Independent valuation fee, which is a third-party valuation for provenance and insurance. This costs about $150 per work.

- Framing/stretching fee necessary for the work to be hung in a rental scenario. This costs about $250 per work.

Rental income is paid monthly and it is guaranteed by the company arranging the rental. After a two- or three-year period, the work is returned to you, but you could renegotiate another rental.

How to invest

Following are some useful guidelines for investing in art:

- Diversify across artists and types of artworks — for example, landscapes and portraits.

- Your investment time horizon should be five to 10 years or even longer, so it is doubly important to buy something you like.

- Do not buy on the news of an artist's passing. This can cause a false market to develop in the short-term, which is not sustainable over the longer term. However, it is often smart to sell on such news because of short-term capital appreciation.

- Do not rely on auctions to obtain a bargain. The prices listed in catalogues are frequently conservative and a bidding war may ensue at an auction. Before attending auctions make sure you have researched the artist and that the pieces you are interested in are authentic.

- Do not blindly follow a crowd. There is a difference between taking advantage of a popular, sustainable trend and merely buying something because everyone else is.

- Beware of buying art at the opening of an exhibition when drinks may be flowing freely and your emotions may rule your head.

- Research the artist before you buy artwork. Assess how prolific they are. Generally the more art they produce, the lower the potential for capital appreciation.

- Look for historical trends of increasing value, but bear in mind that for many artists there may be no discernible price histories.

- Do not buy on impulse if you are out to make a profit.

- Make sure you authenticate an artwork. This is especially important with an expensive purchase.

- If you see an artwork that you like but cannot afford, politely make your best offer. The seller can only say no.

- Always remember that your aim with investment collecting is to make a profit and buying artwork should be treated like any other investment decision.

Fascinating collectables ...

Rare ceramics and pottery

In Australia ceramics and pottery are synonymous with Marguerite Mahood, William Ricketts, Grace Secombe and Philippa James. Marguerite Mahood was born in Melbourne in 1901 and she studied drawing at the National Gallery School. She became a painter before turning to ceramics and her first solo exhibitions were held in Melbourne and in Sydney in the 1930s. Mahood died in 1989. Until 2005 few of her pieces came onto the market, so collectors could not acquire them and there was basically no secondary market. However, in 1997 nine pieces were listed in one auction and shortly afterwards a major collector sold his entire holdings of 50 ceramic pieces. This collector also sold 50 other items of Mahood's, including drawings and watercolours. In the sales of the late 1990s some high prices were paid for Mahood's work, including a renaissance bust dated circa 1930 ($9500) and a female face mask with a Marlene Dietrich theme ($19500).

Philippa James is a leading name in pottery in Australia and some people collect her work exclusively. James originates from Melbourne and nowadays her jugs sell for $500 to $5000. Typical of James's work is an 11 centimetre jug dated circa 1935, which today is worth $900. A 17 centimetre jug with an applied gumnut leaf is valued at $1400. In October 2009 the highest price fetched at a Leonard Joel auction in Melbourne was for a 16 centimetre vase with applied gumleaf that sold for $3300. Six months earlier a 1923 earthenware vase with moulded cicada and leaf decoration sold for just under $7000.

Wine

Seasoned wine collectors believe that the best approach is to drink some of it as time goes by. Firstly, this adds to the enjoyment of wine collecting and, secondly, it enables you to experience firsthand the maturation of your wine. Generally speaking fine wine improves with age, so you would expect a portfolio of good wine to increase in quality, and therefore value, as time goes by. However, there is always the possibility that the maturation process will go too far and the wine will 'go off'. You can monitor this periodically by drinking some of your wine, although you have to take the cost of monitoring your investment into your purchase and sale price. For example, if you buy a dozen wines for $20 per bottle and hold them for 10 years, over which time the price per bottle increases to $50 per bottle, you can confidently drink 50 per cent of the bottles over that time and still make a profit when you sell. While the intention is not to consume collectables, the regular tasting of wines you collect is not only enjoyable but is even recommended! So if you wish to be a wine collector and investor, how should you go about investing in wine to maximise profit?

The business of investing in wine for profit is much better developed in Europe than it is in Australia. In the UK and Europe good records are kept of the potential profits that can be made from investing in wine. For example, wine brokers Fine+Rare have been compiling records on wine investments since 2004. In December of that year a case of Chateau Lafite Rothschild vintage 2000 cost UK£2560. By September 2010 it was worth UK£18400, an increase of 611 per cent in six years. Somewhat less spectacular is a case of Chateau Petrus vintage 2000, which cost UK£12000 a case in December 2004 and was worth UK£24627 a case in September 2010. However, this is still an increase of 255 per cent over six years.

The *en primeur* system allows wine enthusiasts to secure cases of wine when the grapes are harvested and the wine ageing process begins, but before the wine is bottled. A buyer makes an initial down payment to secure a case(s) and makes the final payment when delivery is due. Chateau Lafite Rothschild vintage 2009 was made available *en primeur* in June 2010 for UK£10000 a case and by September it was worth UK£13657 a case, an increase of 36 per cent in three months prior even to its release.

A major drawback when investing in wine is the special storage facilities it requires. The ideal is to store wine in a dark in-ground cellar where the temperature varies between 12 and 15 degrees Celsius with humidity between 65 and 70 per cent and there should be no vibrations. The alternatives to this include storing it off site with a company that specialises in wine storage, or buying a wine cabinet, which takes up a good deal of space. The cost of a wine cabinet that will house 500 bottles is about $7500.

Did you know ... When it comes to champagne magnums attract a premium price, and some collectors keep nothing else. In June 2008, three magnums of Dom Perignon (vintages 1966, 1973 and 1976) sold for a total of US$97 937 in New York.

How to invest

An academic study done in 2007 for the American Association of Wine Economists on investing in wine in Australia and the UK found that the long-term after-tax return from investing in Australian wine of all vintages after transaction, storage and insurance costs was between 5 per cent and 6 per cent per annum. This is not high when you take inflation into account. However, it was found that if an investor focused on the top vintages of Australian wine (including 1986, 1990 and 1994), as well as other more recent good years, the equivalent return after-tax was 9.3 per cent per annum. With a little research it is not difficult to establish the better years for wine in Australia and to structure your cellar accordingly. (For more details, check <www.wine-economics.org/workingpapers/AAWE_WP06.pdf>.)

Following are some useful guidelines for investing in wine:

- Red wine in the bottle improves better with age than white wine, so have more reds than whites, depending on your own drinking preferences.

- Talk to a knowledgeable independent retailer. Tastes differ but their advice is free.

- Never buy less than two bottles of a wine. Then when you drink one, you have some idea of how good (or bad) the others will be. Earmark a part of your cellar for resale, but buy multiple bottles of these wines so that you can try them yourself.

- It is always better to sell a wine too young rather than too old, so do not buy a dozen bottles of wine and put them away indefinitely. Monitor their progress and then you will know their resale appeal.

- You do not need a lot of money to acquire fine wines. One way to minimise costs is by buying mixed lots at wine auctions. Other collectors may tend to focus on dozen bottle lots of the same wine.

- Do not buy solely with profit in mind. Rather, buy good-quality wines that you would like to drink and sell the excess after two to 15 years of cellaring as advised by the winemaker and as taste and markets dictate. A useful rule of thumb is not to buy a wine without first trying it because nothing beats your own taste and judgement.

- Points of sale include wine auctions, retailers and newspapers, depending on how much wine you have to sell, its price and its quality. But the first step is to acquire a good cellar of wines that will improve in the bottle.

Stamps

The world's first stamps were issued in the UK in 1840 and stamp collecting is said to have begun one year later. Today there are an estimated 30 million stamp collectors in the world. Postage stamps are an underrated investment. They are portable and tangible and they have good profit potential. Most investment collectors start a stamp collection as a hobby and seek to make profits later on. In terms of weight, a stamp is potentially the most valuable collectable you can buy. For example, a Great Britain Penny Black in exceptional condition, which weighs just one-tenth of a gram (and which originally cost only one British penny), was recently sold for around US$385 000.

It is generally true that an unused stamp is worth more than the same stamp used. For example, it is estimated that an unused set of eight Hawaiian Missionary Stamps is today worth US$100 000, but worth much less if used. There are sometimes exceptions to this rule, such as inaugural flight airmail letters which had a used stamp and the envelope signed by the pilot. Some very high prices are paid for rare stamps in high-quality condition and this serves to exclude most people from the market. Fortunately, there are myriad other stamp collecting opportunities available on a smaller scale and investing in them can pay dividends.

Stamps of all types are in high demand and the secondary markets for them are lively. You can expect many stamps to appreciate in value after as little as four years. However, an old stamp is not necessarily valuable. Rarity, condition and demand are much more important. For example, an Australian stamp printed more than 50 years ago with a kangaroo on the front might be considered 'old', but in some cases hundreds of millions of these stamps were issued and their value today is less than $A1.

In some cases an historical event will cause the value of stamps of a particular kind to take off. For example, stamps depicting Princess Diana sold on eBay for 10 times their original value after her death. Of course no-one could have predicted this event in advance, but in other respects you can adopt a scientific approach to stamp collecting with a view to making a profit at the same time.

One of the advantages of stamp collecting is that they are in everyday use in all parts of the world and you can specialise in particular themes, such as countries, monarchs or eras.

Did you know ...

Forgers are often at work with stamps and postmarks. One trick is to turn an unused stamp without any gum on the back, which is worth considerably less, into a stamp with a (forged) fine postmark.

Stamp dealers

There are many hundreds of stamp dealers throughout Australia and choosing one to advise you on your collection is the single most important decision you will make. For this reason it is wise to obtain a diverse range of opinions from several different dealers, at least three or four. Word of mouth is a good way of locating a stamp dealer but failing that there are other things you can do.

Following are issues you should address with a dealer you propose trading with:

- The extent to which they focus on collecting for investment purposes.

- The types of stamps they carry and their view on the potential of those stamps for capital appreciation.

- The length of time they have been in business.

- The scope for selling your purchases back to the dealer and their buy/sell spread.

- Their knowledge of trade fairs, exhibitions, auctions, other dealers, collecting clubs and the overall market for stamps in your price category.

- Their willingness to devote time to discussing your collection and your investment goals regardless of how much business you do with them.

- Whether they will store stamps under optimal environmental conditions, and if so, how often you can view your collection and for what fee.

- Whether they can arrange insurance, and if so, the cost.

- Their sources of supply and whether they have access to overseas stamps of investment quality.

- The extent of their valuing expertise; for example, do they have a history of providing expert valuations in the field of stamp collecting?

- Do they have an established base of investment collector clients?

You should get to know several dealers, as the time you spend discussing your collection and your investment goals with them will be worthwhile from a strategic point of view.

How to invest

Following are some useful guidelines when planning your investment strategy:

- If you already have a collection, make sure it is organised. At the very least, sort by country and approximate chronological order. A dealer can then assess the value of your collection more easily.

- Buy a quality stamp catalogue that will provide you with information about different stamp types, the rarity of stamps and their approximate market value. Some recognised stamp catalogues that have an international reputation are Stanley Gibbons, Michel, Minkus, Scott and Yvert et Tellier. Some catalogues have both printed and online versions and one subscription covers both.

- To be a savvy stamp investment collector you will need knowledge of how to classify, grade and certify stamps, as well as an understanding of stamp dealers, stamp storage and stamp handling. You will also need to know stamp collecting conventions. Start small and learn these skills as you go.

- Beware of a dealer who might be trying to offload their own stamps onto you, especially if they have experienced difficulties selling them in the past.

- Based on a study undertaken by Salomon Brothers Investment Bank in 1997, the return from investing in stamps in the 83 years prior to 1990 was 10 per cent per annum before tax.

- You can commence a stamp collection with $500, from where you can add stamps as your financial circumstances permit. However, you will need $5000 or more to invest in a broad portfolio of investment grade stamps from which you can earn an acceptable return.

- Stamps are not recession proof because during a downturn investors have less to spend and demand falls.

Coins

There is a greater number of valuable coins in existence than there are valuable stamps, but you need more capital to take advantage of this. And the most valuable coins are worth a good deal more than the most valuable stamps. A world record price for a coin was set in 2010 when the finest of about 140 known examples of a US 'Flowing Hair Silver Dollar' of 1794 sold for US$7.85 million. The coin was last sold in 2003 in a private sale for what was believed to be several million US dollars and prior to that it was sold in New York in 1984 for US$264 000.

There is still money to be made from investing in coins on a smaller scale. Table 2.1 shows the recent increase in capital value of a selection of Australian coins.

Table 2.1: increase in value of selected Australian coins, 2000 to 2010

Type of coin	Year	Grade	2000 ($)	2010 ($)
Florin	1953	Proof	5 000	45 000
Sixpence	1938	Proof	2 725	25 000
Penny	1927	Proof	10 600	85 000
Threepence	1926	Proof	4 450	45 000
Colonial Dump	1813	Fine	5 500	25 000

Source: Coinworks Pty Ltd.

Note that table 2.1 does not reveal the coins that exhibited the greatest percentage increase in capital value. For example, a 1919–1921 Pattern Kookaburra Type 1 increased from a value of $40 000 in 2000 to $550 000 in 2010.

The return you can expect from investing in rare coins will vary depending on the coins, as is evident from table 2.1. Numerous studies have been undertaken on the average annual return from investing in a portfolio of rare coins for periods as long as 80 years. For example, based on an auction at Spink & Son Ltd, London, in 2003 it was found that a selection of 50 coins had appreciated in value by 10.5 per cent per annum over a 53-year period. More recently it has been found that the 13-year returns to 2009 of selected rare coins were in the order of 11 per cent per annum, but the range of returns could vary from as low as 7 per cent per annum to as high as 18 per cent per annum. Note that this period included the global financial crisis during which time prices remained stable or even fell. Promoters of rare coin investments in Australia freely quote returns of 13 per cent to 14 per cent per annum or more, but 10 per cent to 11 per cent per annum is probably more accurate.

Did you know ... A fossicker with a metal detector in Victoria found a rare 1855 Queen Victoria half sovereign made at the long-defunct Sydney mint. Despite spade damage on the reverse rim it is worth around $30 000.

Gold bullion

Investing in rare coins needs to be distinguished from investing in gold bullion coins, such as the South African Krugerrand. The point of investing in gold bullion coins, which are 99 per cent gold bullion, is to gain exposure to gold, and their value will fluctuate in accordance with movement of gold prices. One of the attractions is that the price of gold, which is always measured in US dollars per ounce, usually moves in the opposite direction to prices in financial markets. Hence when the sharemarket falls dramatically, as happened during the global financial crisis, the price of gold normally increases. On the other hand, when the sharemarket is booming gold is neglected. It is the counter-cyclical nature of gold that is appealing to many investors.

However, over the very long term the upswings and downswings in the price of gold balance out, so the overall return from investing in gold using a buy and hold strategy is negligible. For example, if you bought gold in 1596 and held it until 1996—that is, for 400 years—you would have derived a return of 0.04 per cent per annum, which would not have made you wealthy. But during that period there were returns during particular years as high as 77.6 per cent for a single year. This compares with a low in the worst year of −28.7 per cent. Fundamentally, the right time to invest in gold is when uncertainty in financial markets abounds, when banks fail, when paper money is debased and when there is a general flight to quality assets.

Other gold bullion coins include the American Eagle, the Austrian Philharmonic, the Chinese Panda and the Canadian Maple Leaf. However, these are generally more expensive than the Krugerrand. It is important to note that the price of rare coins usually doesn't increase, even if they have a gold component, because investors will have less to spend and demand will fall.

Numismatic dealers

As with stamp collecting, it is imperative that you team up with a good coin dealer if you are serious about making money from rare coin investing.

When assessing a numismatist you should apply much the same criteria as when evaluating a stamp dealer. Indeed many numismatists also deal in stamps as well as banknotes, medals, tokens and memorabilia. The main thing to be concerned about is the dealer's ability to provide you with sound advice in terms of coins to buy and sell irrespective of the coins they stock themselves. Ask about selling coins back to them and their buy/sell spread and gauge their knowledge of auction processes and prices.

Did you know ... Probably the most well-known valuable Australian coin is a 1930 George V Penny in very fine condition. It was worth one penny in 1930 and by 1967 it was worth $510. After that its value took off and by the end of 2008 it was worth $50 000.

How to invest

Following are some useful guidelines when investing in coins:

- There are an estimated two million coin collectors in the world, which is fewer by far than the number of stamp collectors.

- You should not begin an investment coin collection with less than $5000, as you will need about that amount to buy a broad portfolio of investment quality coins that have the potential to increase in value.

- Buy a selection of 10 to 20 different coins to prevent an undue reliance on a particular coin.

- You can buy coins from dealers and at auction. 'Mint product' can be purchased directly from places such as the Royal Perth Mint.

- The state of preservation of a coin — that is, its condition — is the main determinant of its price and saleability. Do not attempt to clean coins because most cleaning methods will result in some abrasion to a coin's surface and reduce its value.

- Plan on a five- to 10-year investment time horizon. If you invest over a shorter time period, buying and selling costs will eat into your profit.

- Some coins are much rarer than others. For example, a Great Britain 1933 penny is rare, as is the 1804 US dollar, the 1919 Australian shilling and the 1921 Canadian 50-cent piece.

- Although a suitable storage environment is more important for stamps than coins, coins should be housed in an airtight seasoned hardwood box that is free of moisture. Coins should not be placed in contact with each other or with any other metal object.

- If you choose to focus on collecting Australian coins, bear in mind that decimal coins — that is, post-1966 — are generally only worth their face value. The exception is the circular 50-cent piece (minted for a short time after the introduction of decimal currency in 1966), as it has a relatively high silver content. Commemorative 50-cent pieces, of which there are numerous versions, are only worth $0.50.

Mint product is available from dealers such as the Rare Coin Company <www.rarecoin.com.au> and Noble Numismatics <www.noble.com.au>.

Banknotes

Banknotes were originally developed in China in the eighth century as a temporary solution to a copper shortage that meant that coins could not be minted. As they are usually made of paper, banknotes need careful storage and they should be preserved in plastic folders. Condition is important and the best banknotes are designated 'Uncirculated' (UNC), which means that they are perfectly preserved and they have never been mishandled, the paper is clean and firm and the corners are sharp and square.

The potential for capital appreciation of rare, Uncirculated banknotes is excellent. For example, an Uncirculated Australian 1936 Riddle/ Sheehan Ten Shilling Note (R11), which has a face value of 10 shillings (half-a-pound), was worth $15 in 1967 and $12750 in December 2008. Over this 41-year period the average return was 17.4 per cent per annum. Similarly, an Uncirculated Australian 1961 Coombs/Wilson One Pound Starnote (R34bs) was worth $10 in 1967 and $37500 in December 2008, an average return of 21.6 per cent per annum. This latter banknote could have been purchased as recently as 1987 for $500, resulting in a profit of $37000 by December 2008 or a return of 7300 per cent for 21 years.

Unlike decimal coins, Uncirculated $1 and $2 banknotes can be valuable. For example an Uncirculated 1966 Coombs/Wilson Two Dollar Type 1 Specimen Note (RDS2) is currently valued at $23500, while a consecutive pair of 'About Uncirculated' (one grade below Uncirculated) 1969 Phillips/Randall One Dollar Starnotes (R73s) is worth around $7000. Starnotes were banknotes produced between 1948 and 1971 to replace other notes that were spoiled in the printing process. They were so called because the last digit of the serial number was an asterisk (or star).

Numismatists deal in both coins and banknotes and, as always, you should seek one that suits your financial circumstances and investment goals. The Australasian Numismatic Dealer's Association (ANDA) is helpful in providing a list of its members, or you may know someone who can recommend a dealer. As with rare coins, a desirable investment time horizon for banknotes is five to 10 years.

Did you know ... A 1934 Riddle/Sheehan Ten Pound Note in Uncirculated condition was worth $27.50 in 1967. Nine years later it was worth $140 and by 2006 it was worth $28 000. It then jumped in value by $10 000 in the next two years to be worth $38 000 in December 2008.

How to invest

Following are some useful guidelines for investing in banknotes:

- You can buy banknotes from dealers and at auction.

- Rarity is important, so ensure you know how many of an item was made before you invest.

- Condition is also important, so pay attention to grading. An otherwise valuable banknote will be heavily discounted if it is in poor condition.

- Always keep banknotes in protective covers.

- Buy from dealers who you expect to be operating in the future, as they may be the best outlet for repurchasing your banknotes. Ask them about their buyback policy when you purchase.

- If in doubt about an investment, get a second opinion.

Collecting books

If you want to become a book collector and investor, a love of literature is a must. Unlike stamps, coins and banknotes, which you can store off site, such as at a bank, books are most likely going to be with you at home and the enjoyment you get from handling them is part of the collecting and investment process.

Books are a different type of collectable from items such as stamps, coins and banknotes because what constitutes 'classic literature' is constantly shifting, while for investment-quality coins or stamps, rarity is measurable and easy to define. Stamps, coins and banknotes are also similar because their markets are well established and determined by the spending power of collectors and investors, while books are like art since their value is much more subjective.

When collecting books a good deal of investment activity centres around first editions of classic works. For example, a first edition of Sir Arthur Conan Doyle's book *The Hound of the Baskervilles* cost UK£1 in 1902, while a copy today in good condition is worth in excess of UK£80 000, representing an average return of 11.8 per cent per annum. A first edition of *Lord of the Rings* by JRR Tolkien published in 1954 cost UK£6 at the time, while today in good condition it is worth around UK£25 000, a return of 18.5 per cent per annum. There is less documentary evidence available relating to the performance of rare books than there is for other collectables such as stamps and coins. However, the long-term return from investing in rare books—that is, over 20 years or more—is in the vicinity of 9 per cent per annum with low volatility.

Apart from first editions there are many other collectable books you can invest in, although there are a few problems you will have to overcome when making your choices. Other than well-known first editions, the markets for rare books are not as sophisticated and reliable as they are for stamps, coins and banknotes. It is more difficult to obtain information on which to base your investment decisions. Also books take up much more space than stamps, coins and banknotes, so you will need to specialise and the potential number of themes is vast. You may simply find that you cannot locate a suitable dealer in your speciality. The internet makes buying and selling books easier—for example, eBay—but it is not a substitute for good hands-on advice. You will need to keep a close watch on the prices of the books in your field as they change hands through dealers, book fairs and auctions, and this information isn't as readily available as it is with other collectables.

Another issue is that condition is vital and to ensure quality you need to view a book before you buy it, which makes purchasing books via the internet dubious. It is difficult, therefore, to do business with someone on the opposite side of the country.

Themes for collecting and investing include early French voyages to Australia, Australian military history, Antarctica, rare Australian art, children's books, Australian trade and corporate histories, Australian crime fiction and Van Diemen's Land Tasmania, to name just a very few. Conceivably there are as many themes as there are investors and finding a dealer who caters to your speciality may be difficult, not to mention finding suitable markets for your books.

Did you know …
A first edition of JK Rowling's book *Harry Potter and the Philosopher's Stone* cost only about $6 in 1997 when it was published but today it is worth around $40 000. It would be worth even more with the author's signature.

How to invest

Following are some useful guidelines for investing in rare books:

- While you can start investing with just one book, you can start a significant investment collection with around $5000 and slowly build up the level of your investment.

- The condition of books is vital and they need to be kept from risks such as household damage, dampness and fire. Repairing very old books is something that should only be done by an experienced professional bookbinder.

- A rare book is much more valuable with its dust cover intact. For this reason it is wise for the dust cover to have a plastic protective cover.

- Books are bulky items and cannot be stored in a safe. Make sure your household contents insurance covers your collection.

- The author's signature in a book will add value, especially if it is a very rare book. With regard to less rare books, it will still add value depending on the popularity of the book.

- For modern books the best strategy is to invest in what you like and collect those books that have been well reviewed, and keep the reviews. Go to book launches and obtain the author's signature when purchasing your copies.

- There is a lively market in out-of-print books in all genres. For example, a book that cost less than $30 when first published 15 years ago may have a current value of more than $100 in the out-of-print market.

- More so than other collectables, rare books go in and out of fashion over short time periods. You will have to accept that a book for which you have paid $1000 or more may go out of fashion quickly. Always diversify your portfolio and only invest in what you like.

- Adopt a 10-year investment time horizon when collecting rare books as they appreciate more slowly than other collectables.

- Always buy hardcover editions in preference to paperbacks and store them on a rigid bookshelf. Because of space limitations and the fact that markets are difficult to research and access, you may decide that investing in rare books is not for you.

Memorabilia

Memorabilia, including military, sport and music, provides many opportunities for collecting and investing. The potential for making money can be combined with your passion for collecting items in a theme and there are a large number of areas in which you can specialise. A good source of information and the opportunity to buy and sell items can be found on eBay <www.ebay.com.au>, which also has numerous buying guides. For example, within the area of 'Music Memorabilia' eBay has the following categories:

- apparel
- original autographs

- reprinted autographs

- concert memorabilia

- framed items

- novelties

- photos and clippings

- pins and buttons

- posters

- publications

- other.

Did you know ... The most valuable sporting memorabilia are those associated with Hall of Fame athletes, limited editions, big events (such as the Soccer World Cup and the Ashes) and items in mint condition. Autographs are popular but only if they are authentic.

However, since there are so many types of memorabilia and multiple themes within each category, markets are fragmented and reliable performance figures are difficult to gauge. For example, it is likely that investing in one military medal will have a vastly different return from investing in another.

It is not essential to begin your collection with expensive items. You can pay a lot of money for some sporting memorabilia, such as a cricket bat signed by Sir Donald Bradman, but other items such as a signed football jersey are much more affordable. With the exception of some military and sporting memorabilia, items are likely to change hands in the hundreds of dollars or less, rather than the thousands of dollars. Memorabilia may therefore be suitable for collecting if you have a low budget.

With regard to historic memorabilia, such as military memorabilia, it is important that items are in good condition and that you know the history behind an item. For example, if you buy a medal, make sure that you know the background to it being awarded.

Did you know ... Memorabilia from the early days of Qantas Airways is increasingly hard to find. A Qantas flight ticket from Blackall to Charleville in 1923 is valued at $700 and this should increase steadily.

How to invest

Following are some useful guidelines for investing in memorabilia:

- Focus on areas that give you enjoyment. Collecting memorabilia should be fun, with the added incentive that you can make a profit if you choose well and have a little luck.

- Internationally recognised items are generally more valuable and saleable than those relating only to Australia as the market for buyers is bigger and demand is greater.

- Make sure that you get what you pay for. If buying over the internet, ensure that an item is accurately described. Where possible obtain a certificate of authenticity.

- As with other kinds of collectables, rarity, condition and demand are the chief determinants of value.

- You need only buy one item of memorabilia to get started, whereas with collectables such as stamps and coins you need a portfolio.

- You can sell memorabilia via the internet. Websites such as eBay are a good way to stay in touch with prices.

- Memorabilia has to be stored appropriately, much the same as stamps, coins, banknotes and books. Avoid dampness, heat, sunlight and household contamination.

- You can buy memorabilia for less than $100 and you should begin with an item that you would like to build on to create a collection. You're likely to have to pay more for an item that is old, so buy a current version with the aim of buying older, more expensive items later.

- Many memorabilia purchases are akin to speculative investments because it is impossible to know what will become fashionable in future years. But if you initially restrict yourself to a purchase of one or two items of around $100 each, the risk is minimised.

Fads, hobbies and obsessions

It should always be borne in mind that you can collect any items you like as a hobby. One man in Canberra who was featured on the ABC television program *Collectors* was fascinated with 'Terroramobilia', which is basically anything related to terror. He has a vast array of posters featuring different aspects of terror as well as novelty items, such as cigarette lighters and ash trays. He also has the name tags from more than 300 conferences that he has attended on terror. It is an impressive collection and it might even be worth something, although the collection is probably unique and therefore difficult to value. Nevertheless, this collector enjoys his hobby and he derives satisfaction from adding to it.

The program featured another collector who owns about 4500 key rings that hang from hooks in his home. He estimates that the hooks alone are worth around $4500. Another guest showed his collection of Coca-Cola cans that commemorate particular events—such as the Sydney Olympics. The message is that you can be a collector of whatever you fancy and depending on what you choose you may be the only person in Australia, or the world, doing it.

To get started, follow your interests and begin in a small way. Tell your friends, work colleagues and relatives about your collection and ask for donations. Getting others involved is half the fun. See if you can find anyone else who is collecting the same items as you. This is not only enjoyable but you may be able to exchange items as well.

When your collection grows you will have to decide how to store and display your items. This is actually one of the things you will need to consider at the time you decide what to collect. It is not a huge issue if you are collecting drink coasters but if you decided to collect old computers, you will need a lot of space to store them. After you have begun to acquire a meaningful collection you will need to consider making purchases to round it out. The size of your budget will also have a bearing on what you collect. What began as a hobby in your spare time may evolve into an obsession that you spend all of your time on, so be considerate of those around you and how it affects them.

Memorabilia such as a lock of Elvis Presley's hair, a dress owned by Princess Diana or a bra owned by Marilyn Monroe doesn't find its way anywhere near Australia. The latter sold at auction in London in July 2009 for US$5200.

How to invest

Following are some useful guidelines for investing as a hobby:

- If you view collecting as a fad, hobby or obsession, have fun while you are pursuing it. Collect what sparks your enthusiasm and fits your budget.

- If you wish to keep an eye on profit, remember that rarity, condition and demand are the key determinants of value.

- Physical factors will impact on what you can realistically collect. For example, you cannot collect classic cars or televisions if you have nowhere to store them.

- Thoroughly research the area in which you specialise; it is part of the enjoyment.

- Take an interest in what other people collect. You will learn from their experiences and make new friends. Discussing your collectables with other people makes for great conversation and facilitates socialising generally.

- Many fads, hobbies and obsessions begin with collecting items that may not cost anything. For example, you may be given an old radio.

- Have an idea of what you will do with a collection when you wish to dispose of it. Selling is a possibility in some cases, but others give their collections to museums.

- Keep in mind that it is unlikely that there is nobody who is collecting what you are — the job is to find them.

- Word of mouth is the best way of selling collectables that have been acquired as part of a fad, hobby or obsession.

Key points

- In general art is an investment for the longer term. Although you could strike it lucky and buy an artwork of an emerging artist that doubles in value in one year, this doesn't usually happen.

- The work of established artists appreciates more slowly but returns are more reliable. However, their artwork is also generally expensive.

- You can earn up to 8 per cent per annum through buying artworks and renting them out, but it is a specialised business and you need good advice to get started. There are several companies that can help you out.

- Creating a wine cellar is an excellent idea if you enjoy wine, but space and storage limitations may adversely affect your plans. Begin in a small way with a few dozen bottles of wine that you can expect to improve in the bottle.

- As with most collectables the time spent acquiring knowledge about wine will pay off. In particular, learn to identify the good vintage years for regions of interest.

- When investing in stamps, coins, banknotes and books, teaming up with a dealer who is sympathetic to your circumstances and financial goals is crucial.

- An old collectable is not necessarily more valuable than a more modern one, except insofar as there may be fewer old collectables in existence because of attrition. The prices for some collectables are influenced by historical events as well as the usual criteria of rarity, condition and demand.

- The condition of collectables is vital, so make sure that you store them properly.

- The markets for stamps, coins and banknotes are well established and obtaining information about them is easier than many other types of collectables.

- Decimal coins are not valuable but decimal notes, notably Uncirculated $1 and $2 notes, can be valuable.

- Do not put all your eggs in one basket. Aim to have a diversified portfolio of collectables both between and within investment categories.

- Special considerations apply to investing in rare books because they are bulky items and you keep them at home. Books also go in and out of fashion more quickly than other collectables.

- Investing in memorabilia is more speculative because of the varying nature of the markets. However, you can obtain items for low prices and the potential returns can be high.

- There are an infinite number of different items you can collect and your choice is limited only by your imagination and resourcefulness. If you wish to keep an eye on profit, remember that rarity, condition and demand are the key determinants of value.

- Invest in those areas that you find interesting and enjoyable.

International markets

For some collectables, such as European art, fine china and glassware, international markets offer much more profitable opportunities than Australian markets. Some collectables are only offered for sale in the UK, Europe, Asia or the US, and if you wish to buy them, you will have to do so overseas. Similarly, if you wish to obtain the best price for these collectables when you sell them, you will also need access to overseas markets.

Buying and selling in overseas markets requires knowledge of these markets and an appreciation of the added difficulties you will face compared with trading in Australia. The internet has revolutionised potential participation in overseas markets but there are still many challenges to overcome. For example, you cannot directly assess the condition of an item via the internet and this is critical in determining its value. This chapter provides helpful information if you wish to buy and sell internationally.

Buying and selling overseas

Before you buy a collectable overseas you should be aware that you will generally also have to sell it overseas to obtain the best price. You cannot realistically buy, say, an English painting in London and then bring it back to Australia and make a substantial profit by selling it here. The Australian market is simply not big enough or deep enough to be able to return the investment. You will find the number of potential buyers for your painting is limited and that you would be foregoing some profits by trying to sell it here. The upshot is that if you buy overseas, you must be prepared to sell overseas and you may decide that it's just is not worth the inconvenience — unless a handsome profit is expected. By trading overseas you will also be subjected to currency risks and you can enter into an otherwise profitable investment that is negated by an adverse movement in exchange rates. You will find more details about this further in this chapter.

An important advantage of buying and selling collectables overseas is the sheer number and range of items available. As you might expect the highest prices for collectables are generally paid overseas, but the expansive nature of the market does not just apply to big ticket items. Some years ago there was an auction in the US of items that belonged to Jacqueline Kennedy Onassis. Everyday household items sold for much more than their face value simply because of their history and who had owned them. If you wanted an item, you had to bid at the auction, which was held in the US. At overseas auctions (and in Australia, too) telephone bidding is possible and also nowadays live internet bidding. The point that needs to be made is that auctions such as this for the possessions of Jacqueline Kennedy Onassis are not held in Australia. You have to buy the items overseas. Similarly, if you wish to sell these items, you will need to dispose of them overseas to obtain the highest price. Naturally, if you just want the enjoyment that comes from owning such an item and you have no intention of ever selling it, you needn't be concerned with liquidating your investment.

Another consideration is that some items that are collected on a small scale in Australia are traded on a much more sophisticated basis overseas. For example, comic strips and comic books may be identified by collectors in Australia as areas where there is scope for capital appreciation and there is a market for these items on eBay. However, overseas there are auction houses that have separate departments that specialise in them. The Parisian auction house Tajan, <www.tajan.com>, held an auction in October 2010 at which an original black and white comic strip (rather than a comic book) by Peyo was expected to bring as much as $64 000. Another original black and white strip by Hugo Pratt was expected to bring as much as $50 000. Such comic strips are not available on eBay.

Considerations when buying art overseas

Many collectables have a unique geographical reference point. For example, if you collect British stamps, the range of stamps available is largest in the UK. Hence, it makes sense to gain access to British dealers and auction houses and if possible attend trade fairs in the UK. Likewise, if you wished to acquire a painting of a local scene of New York, Paris, Macau or London, the biggest markets for these paintings may be in their respective countries. There is a large number of emerging artists in these countries, so you needn't pay a lot of money—for example, less than $1000—but at the same time you need to be sure that you get what you pay for and that your purchases are delivered to you in good condition.

When buying the work of an overseas artist you need to be concerned with the same sorts of issues as when buying Australian art. Following are useful guidelines:

- Set your objectives.

- Determine your budget.

- Formulate an investment strategy.

- Research artists and genres so that you know what you are buying.

- Take a long-term view; for example, five to 10 years.

- Have a balanced portfolio—that is, do not put all your eggs in one basket.

- Buy something you like because the chances are you will own it for some years.

- Monitor the progress of your portfolio.

 Doyle New York has auctioned the estates of Hollywood stars, including James Cagney, Gloria Swanson, Bette Davis, Rock Hudson and Ruth Gordon, as well as musicians such as Louis Armstrong, Duke Ellington and Count Basie.

Aesthetic appeal

As with any purchase of art it is important that the artwork appeals to you because you may be looking at it for a long time. The aesthetic appeal of overseas art is most easily established through photos which galleries, and artists themselves, make available to you. Note the dimensions of an artwork you are interested in and whether it is framed or unframed. A good photo is an accurate way of portraying a painting's aesthetic appeal and you should be able to determine if you will be happy owning the painting and displaying it in your home or elsewhere. Ideally, it is best to see a painting in real life before you buy it but this may not be practicable, especially where a small amount of money is involved.

Availability

Identifying the artwork that is available in overseas countries is much easier for residents of those countries than it is for someone in Australia. As is the case in Australia, artists hold exhibitions at which paintings are offered for sale and local residents can attend these exhibitions and also visit galleries. For someone in Australia the easiest means by which a purchase can be made is via the internet, but an obvious danger is that of fraud. Many overseas galleries and artists display paintings on the internet and to avoid the risk of a scam it is important that you only deal with people you trust. Hence, you should thoroughly research a gallery or artist before you decide to enter business with them. If you can't find any information on them after a Google search, it is best to look elsewhere, as there are many reputable galleries and artists with whom you can do business. When deciding between approaching a gallery or approaching an artist directly, it is preferable to deal with the artist because then you can avoid paying a commission.

Authentication

A Certificate of Authenticity (CoA) is a must when buying art overseas. If you're making an expensive purchase, it is important to arrange for an expert to authenticate the work as well. This adds considerably to the expense of a purchase, but it is what you would do if making a sizeable art investment in Australia. There are numerous dealer associations in various countries that will do this for you for a fee and some of them are outlined in the 'Useful resources' section at the end of the book. A CoA is issued by an artist and attests to the fact that the painting to which it relates is their own work. It can be important if you ever wish to sell the painting, and doubly so if it is an emerging artist and if the value of their work takes off.

Condition

The condition of a collectable of any type is one of the key determinants of its value. Unless a work is something such as an Old Master or a famous French Impressionist, a painting that you are considering purchasing should be in pristine condition and this is difficult to establish before purchasing with just a photograph. Again, if it is an expensive purchase, it is wise to have an expert assess its condition. If a painting is framed, the frame should also be in excellent condition. Otherwise buy it unframed and have it framed in Australia. It is essential that a painting is shipped in proper packaging, which is another expense you will have to consider. The seller will not take responsibility for damage caused in transit, so you cannot send a painting back. You will need to be sure that the seller has taken every care to preserve your painting when they organise delivery.

Demand

Demand for a collectable is another key determinant of its value. This is a tricky criterion to evaluate when it comes to overseas art because opposing forces are at work. On the one hand, as has already been pointed out, overseas markets are significantly larger than Australian markets so the demand for collectables that have international appeal is much stronger overseas. On the other hand, there is a much greater supply of overseas art in the country of origin so demand and supply can cancel each other out.

For example, there are far more New York City scenes in the US than there are in Australia, but the stronger demand in the large US market is satisfied by its increased supply and the two phenomena serve to keep prices low. In Australia, if an oil painting on canvas of New York City came up for auction, which is not as likely to happen here as in the US, it is conceivable that there may be some buyers who were interested. This in turn would push the price up, reflecting the relative scarcity of such a painting in the Australian market. However, it is also possible that not many people would be interested in the painting, in which case the price fetched would probably be low. Much depends on the circumstances of the auction, as the same painting may sell for a vastly different price at two different events; however, this is unlikely to happen if the painting was auctioned in the US.

Potential for capital growth

When you assess the potential for capital appreciation of an overseas work of art you need to do so in the context of the market in which you bought it. As a starting point you will need to know something about the artist and how the painting you are interested in fits in with the artist's other work. This may be difficult as the artist may be relatively unknown and you will therefore have to rely on the opinions of others. Bear in mind that even local experts, such as valuers and dealers, may not know the artist either, so you may be none the wiser. In the end it may come down to buying a painting simply because you like it without knowing much about its potential for capital appreciation, even after attempting to source this information. Here the usual criteria of not spending too much money and not overcommitting yourself to any one particular artist applies.

Price

The prices of overseas paintings are much the same as they are in Australia, with the exception that at the top of the range you can pay many millions of dollars. Prices generally start at around a couple of hundred dollars and extend into many thousands of dollars or, as mentioned, millions. The buyer pays delivery charges, such as freight, packaging and insurance, which may make a purchase at the low end of this range uneconomical. Some buyers of inexpensive overseas art have been known to entrust the postal service with delivery and dispensed with insurance with good results. Prices are generally quoted in British pounds, euros or US dollars, and you will need to factor in the costs of currency conversion and related charges. The seller will require payment upfront, which usually won't be a problem if they have a good reputation but it may be a concern if they are hitherto unknown.

Liquidity

If you are the owner of a painting purchased overseas, you may be able to dispose of it easily in Australia or you may not. Apart from the usual uncertainty surrounding the secondary market for art, you will need to be concerned about the propensity of buyers to purchase an overseas work of art by a possibly unknown artist. The more information you have about the painting you wish to sell and the artist the better, so keep this in mind when you buy it. Avoid making a forced sale—for example, at auction—so that you can offer a painting again at a later time if the need arises. The rule about generally being obliged to sell a foreign painting overseas in order to obtain the best price still applies. Note also that it might be uneconomical to ship an inexpensive painting overseas for sale as freight, packaging and insurance will eat up your profits.

Buying collectables overseas

When buying collectables overseas you basically have three choices:

- You can buy directly from the owner in a private sale.

- You can buy from a dealer.

- You can buy through an auction house.

Fascinating collectables ...

Vintage model trains

The classic toy train market is large (especially in the US) and there is a global network of collectors and dealers. In Australia the most common manufacturer is Hornby, which makes trains on a much smaller scale than its US counterpart Lionel, which first started making trains in 1900. A Lionel locomotive and tender can be as long as 63.5 centimetres and passenger cars can be 45.7 centimetres. Lionel trains are popular and they are also available in Australia, but the company's golden era was from 1929 to 1969. In the 1950s only a few shops imported Lionel model trains into Australia and only the wealthy could afford them for their children. Nowadays you can begin collecting a Lionel train set for as little as US$400 so prices are not outrageously expensive, but classic trains are a different case. One vintage locomotive can be priced at thousands of dollars on its own.

Lionel catalogues are also in demand by collectors. They were given away at no cost to retailers and now sell for about $50. A classic 1950s passenger car that measures 38.1 centimetres in O gauge, of which you would need five to six units, sells today for around $150.

Another one of the classic US trains is Lionel's die-cast model of the 1938 New York Central Hudson. In 1938 a new model cost US$75, while today in good condition it is worth about US$2500. For any classic train you contemplate buying, you can add a significant amount to its value if it is packaged in its original box.

The range of collectables you can acquire overseas is vast, although as you might expect, buying small-value items — for example, under $200 — is usually uneconomical unless you wish to round out a collection. As a first step in making an overseas purchase you should seek to establish whether there is a dealer association catering to your area of specialisation. For something less obvious, such as Disneyland memorabilia, you wouldn't expect a dealer association to exist. But for more mainstream areas, such as art, stamps, coins, banknotes, wine, gold, diamonds, books and antiques, they do exist. These associations can be useful in leading you to a dealer who can advise you on your purchases (and sales).

Private sale

The main problem with buying from an owner in a private sale is locating someone who has the object that you wish to buy. This is difficult enough if you wish to buy an object in Australia but the task is made even more difficult if the potential vendor is in another country. This is an option that is best avoided unless you can make a visit to the country in question and attend trade fairs and circulate among like-minded collectors and investors. However, some associations foster this process by encouraging their members to communicate among themselves and in this way buyers and sellers can be brought together via their own contact. For example, one of the advantages of being a member of the International Bank Note Society (IBNS), <www.theibns.org>, which is based in the US, is that members receive a directory with contacts and dealers who they can use to increase their collections. The IBNS has a worldwide presence with a network of more than 1750 members in more than 90 countries.

Dealers and auctioneers

There are many dealers and auctioneers overseas who you can access in the interests of investment collecting. Initially you can approach an association or society to find a suitable contact (some of the better-known ones are listed in this book in 'Useful resources'). Bear in mind that associations, societies and auction houses promote their own members or services, so you won't get an unbiased view. Also, many of them are large and do not cater for small investors. This is particularly so with international enquiries. For example, numerous items exchange hands for tens of millions of dollars overseas and if your item is worth only $1000, you are better off selling it in Australia. On the other hand, if you had a European painting to sell, you could contact a major auction house in Australia that has sale rooms in London or Europe and they would ship it there for you.

The best way to contact an overseas dealer or auction house is through their website, which usually contains their address and telephone details. You can also see which services they provide from their website.

Did you know ... World renowned auction house, Christies, began in London in 1766 with a sale of two chamber pots, a pair of sheets, two pillowcases and four irons. In 1970 Christies auctioned the first work of art to sell for over UK£1 million—Velazquez's *Portrait of Juan de Pareja*, which sold for UK£2.3 million. Christies also auctions less conventional collectables. In 1997 Christies sold 79 dresses from the Collection of Diana, Princess of Wales, for US$3 258 750.

Trade fairs

Overseas trade fairs are an excellent way to view collectables firsthand and to see what you like within your price range. There are numerous trade fares for art, sculpture, coins, banknotes and stamps in all parts of the world, and they can be incorporated into overseas trips. At a trade fair, exhibitors display their wares and you can buy them or make contact with a seller for future dealing. Trade fairs also attract buyers and sellers from other areas, sometimes from all over the world depending on the trade fair. Frequently a trade fair will go on for days and they are an excellent way of meeting like-minded collectors. Art fairs are very popular, but in addition there is a wide variety of fairs covering other collectables. The best way to find out about them is to visit the websites of associations, dealers and auction houses.

Foreign exchange considerations

If you invest in collectables overseas, you can make a profit or loss on currency exchange rates as well as a gain or loss on movements in intrinsic capital value. This is best illustrated by an example. Say you purchased a first edition book in the US for US$4000 in March 2000 when the exchange rate was around $A1 = US$0.61. Your outlay would have been A$6557 (ignoring nominal fees for a bank draft). Assume that the value of the book increased by about 7.5 per cent per annum for 10 years and that it was worth US$8000 in the US in 2010. This is a profitable investment, but in 2010 the value of the US dollar was a lot less than in 2000.

For argument's sake, assume that the exchange rate is now A$1 = US$1 — that is, parity—so that the book is now worth A$8000. This is a profit of only A$1443 or less than 2 per cent per annum and you have done a lot worse than an American investor of the same book. Due to an adverse movement in exchange rates, the value of the book in Australian dollars hasn't increased significantly, and the increase was in fact less than the rate of inflation in Australia.

The situation works in reverse. If the value of the Australian currency had declined over the same period, you would be much better off. Also, if there was a market for the book in Australia and its value increased by 7.5 per cent per annum within Australia, the book would be worth around A$13 000 today. However, as discussed earlier in this chapter, you cannot rely on there being a market for the book in Australia. You may be lucky but you may not be. Bear in mind also that another collector who was interested in the book could now buy it in the US for A$8000, so why would they buy it from you in Australia for A$13 000? The message is that when you invest in collectables overseas you need to have a view of what is likely to happen to the Australian dollar.

Did you know ... In the 1960s many popular television programs were westerns. One such program was *Rawhide*, which starred a young Clint Eastwood. The 1961 TV Annual from *Rawhide* is considered a classic and is worth more than $100 today in good condition.

Key points

- Buying and selling collectables overseas is more practicable than ever because of the widespread use of the internet, but the need for a personal inspection of some items still exists.

- The chief attraction of dealing overseas is the enormous size of international markets. There are many collectables bought and sold overseas that do not otherwise find their way to Australia.

- If you buy overseas, you will ordinarily have to sell overseas to obtain the best price. This especially applies to expensive items.

- Contact with associations and societies is a good way to become informed about the markets for collectables, and they provide an avenue for determining the prices being paid.

- Dealers and auction houses will often give you informal advice over the telephone.

- You will need to form a view of the likely fluctuations in the Australian dollar if you buy and sell overseas because any movement will affect your potential profits.

4

Caring for and displaying collectables

This chapter examines what you need to consider when caring for and storing collectables, and also what you need to keep in mind when displaying them in your home or elsewhere. The chapter also looks at the types of insurance you should consider to safeguard your collectable investments. From both an investment and aesthetic point of view, it is important that collectables are handled with care because tears, scratches, marks and other imperfections can significantly reduce their value. In reality, most people do not have the time or resources to care for collectables in the same way as a museum. However, there are some basic guidelines for care, storage and display that you can follow to maximise the value and enjoyment of your collectables.

Collectables are made from a wide variety of materials and often they are composed of more than one material. Consequently, careful thought needs to be taken on what care is appropriate. For example, a clock may be comprised of a wooden case, moving metal parts, ceramic hands and a glass cover. The clock may also have a varnish finish or be painted or coloured in some other way.

The most destructive forces

All materials tend to change over time. It is not possible to prevent this from occurring completely but it is possible to influence how quickly it happens. Some materials age in particular ways simply because of the inherent properties of the material, while others deteriorate because of environmental conditions.

You should be aware that light, temperature and humidity are the main environmental conditions you have to watch out for. Light can damage collectables, even if it is artificial light and you should test for this. Temperatures should remain cool and even, and humidity should be maintained at about 50 per cent. It is easy to neglect these factors if you are not focussed on them, but they are essential when caring for your collectables.

Light

Light, especially direct sunlight, has the potential to harm almost any type of collectable, but this is particularly so with regard to organic materials, such as wood, paper and textiles. Many materials used to make collectables are susceptible to chemical reactions that occur naturally over time and harsh light can speed up the process. In addition, light can dry out materials and result in the fading of colours in prints and fabrics. All collectables should be stored away from direct sunlight, as even objects that may seem to be indestructible, such as plastics, can melt when exposed to direct sunlight. Lights in display cabinets should be used with caution as they can also have a detrimental effect. However, such lights can be beneficial for drying surrounding air when it is damp.

Light levels can be tested with light meters, which can be purchased at photo supply shops. Fluorescent tubes that are low in ultraviolet light should be used wherever possible. Light levels should not exceed 75uW/lumen and lights should be turned off whenever possible, especially in storage areas. Collectables should not be stored or displayed near windows, but if this cannot be avoided, the windows should be covered with curtains or blinds.

When plastics become overheated they give off vapours, which can cause chemical reactions in other materials and damage collectables.

Temperature

The ideal temperature for housing collectables is between 18 and 20 degrees Celsius, which is on the cooler side and may be difficult to maintain on a permanent basis. Depending on where you live, temperatures in summer are likely to be considerably higher than this and trying to maintain such a temperature indoors could cost thousands of dollars per year. Should you have one or two rooms in your home that tend to be cooler than the rest year-round, they are the ideal place for storing and displaying collectables. Generally, hallways or dimly lit rooms are relatively cool and make good areas for fragile items such as paper and textiles. You should avoid areas with extreme temperature fluctuations, such as attics and garages, especially for collectables made of wood, paper and textiles.

You should only move collectables from areas of one temperature level to another gradually. Collectables can suffer damage if moved from a hot to a cold environment or the other way around too quickly. For example, tiny cracks in the glaze of ceramics, called 'crazing', occur naturally but they can appear more quickly when a collectable is exposed to rapid temperature changes.

Humidity

The ideal level for humidity is about 50 per cent. If humidity is too high, metal items can become rusted and mould can grow on items such as wood, paper and textiles. Also a highly humid environment fosters the breeding of insects. On the other hand, when humidity is not high enough, items such as paintings, wood and paper can shrink and crack and become brittle. Humidity levels can be checked by using a hygrometer, which you can buy at many hardware stores. If you live in a very dry area, you can buy a humidifier, which adds moisture to the air.

Handling

To maintain the condition of collectables it is necessary to avoid excessive handling. Some rare collectables are very valuable so they should be handled with extreme care, such as with gloves. The Office of the National Archives of Australia recommends the following:

- Remember how the item was packed so that you can repack it the same way.

- It is best to wear lint-free cotton gloves but failing this ensure that your hands are clean and dry.

- Do not clean objects of archival quality with commercial cleaners. If you must clean them, simply wipe them over with a dry soft cloth or brush gently.

- When packing broken items make sure that the broken edges do not come into contact with each other.

- Do not try to glue any damaged pieces, as the repair of broken collectables should be left to professional restorers.

Note that if a collectable comes in a box, make sure you keep the original packaging as it will add value to the collectable if you ever decide to sell it.

Did you know ...

Care needs to be taken when opening a boxed item. Always try to store the box in a cupboard so that its colour does not fade and damage to it can be avoided.

Many collectables can be cleaned by using a damp cloth, but use distilled water to dampen the cloth because chemicals and minerals in tap water can stain some materials. Other useful cleaning items include soft-bristled brushes for dusting loose particles. Possibilities include shaving brushes, artists' brushes and soft painting brushes. Cans of moisture-free compressed air, which can be purchased from office supply shops, are handy, as are cotton swabs and acid-free tissues. Dry-cleaning may be appropriate for some soiled materials, but if this does not work you could use distilled water to wet clean instead. Isopropyl alcohol is also helpful for cleaning many ceramics and porcelain pieces with glazed finishes, but be careful because alcohol can take the finish off wood and remove painting on glass. Avoid using detergents because anything containing bleach will damage fragile items.

Packaging

Before placing an item in protective packaging it is important to ensure that the object is free of dust, mould, insects and corrosion. Affected items should be separated from your collection, and advice should be sought from an expert restorer or conservator on how to deal with these items. Items tend to be of varying sizes and shapes and may become damaged simply because of their awkwardness. Such items do not fit neatly into drawers or on shelves and it is not always possible to box them. These items are often made from fragile materials and are difficult to retrieve, so damage can occur. Following are specific National Archives of Australia guidelines for such items:

- Wrap items individually so that they do not touch and damage each other.

- Use shock-absorbing packaging materials, such as acid-free tissue, archival foams and bubble pack. Do not use newspaper because the print can be superimposed on collectables.

- Use acid-free boxes. These are available commercially in both standard and custom-made sizes.

- Clearly label items and boxes, but do not write or stick anything directly onto an item's surface. A useful option is to tie a label to the item with cotton thread.

- If an item is too large for a box, drape it with cotton dustsheets.

- Items should only be transported in their protective packaging.

- Textiles should be handled differently from most other items. They should be laid out flat in a box and interleaved with acid-free tissue paper. Folds in textiles should be padded out with a sausage-shaped tissue roll. Natural fibres can be very fragile so you should take care not to crush textiles under a heavy load.

Fascinating collectables ...

Pot lids

In the latter half of the 19th century there was a fad for collecting decorative pot lids in the UK. These ceramic lids were produced by the Staffordshire potteries and were roughly 7 centimetres to 15 centimetres in diameter. They housed such products as paste, pâté and cosmetics. Most lids were mass produced and featured historical events and military campaigns. A few were released as limited editions and depicted special events. For example, one showed George Washington crossing the Delaware River. This particular one is rare and some from this edition have sold for as much as US$4000 in the US.

Being an inherently British collectable, there are not many examples in Australia, although a large collection was auctioned in Melbourne in 2010. The value of pot lids varies from a small, 7-centimetre novelty pot lid produced in the mid-19th century worth $250 up to a group of Prattware lids depicting 19th-century British scenes worth thousands of dollars. In between, a 14.5-centimetre lid revealing a 19th-century street scene by Cauldon is worth $500 and a rare lid showing Queen Victoria on her balcony by Prattware is worth about $750.

Since 1900 there have been a couple of other spurts in activity in the pot lid market. In the late 1960s there was a boom that was consistent with heightened interest in Victoriana, and there was another resurgence in the early 1990s when pot lids brought good prices at auction. Nowadays the market is uncertain and realistically you will need to have access to the British market if you wish to become involved.

Caring for jewellery

The variety of items that you can collect is endless and the steps you should take to care for them depends on factors such as their composition, whether they are 'in use' items and how fragile they are, as well as factors that contribute to their deterioration over time, to name just a few considerations. This section looks at the care of jewellery to highlight just one type of collectable that requires special attention.

Gold, silver and platinum, along with precious or semi-precious stones, are probably the most common materials that jewellery is made from, but jewellery can also be made from shells, ceramics, glass, enamel and copper or copper alloys. Basically any material that can be turned into a pin or bead has been used to make jewellery at some time. From time to time the issue is raised: should very rare jewellery be worn? There is always the risk of loss or damage if jewellery is worn, so anything considered 'priceless' is best left at home; however, pearls need to be worn to maintain their lustre. Ancient jewellery can be deceiving because it may look strong and in good condition but its metal may have become weak and brittle, so it is best left at home as well.

Antique jewellery is wearable, but before you do so check that pins, clasps and safety chains are in good condition and that any stones are kept firmly in place. If you are in doubt, ask a conservator who specialises in archaeological metalwork.

As noted earlier, all collectables are subject to natural deterioration but jewellery is one collectable that is more stable than most other types. The biggest risk is wear and tear through use. For example, stones and enamel can be chipped, clasps and pins may break, and surfaces can become scratched. Also, metals such as silver and copper tarnish and jewellery can become dirty; for example, rings can be affected by soap and earrings and necklaces can be affected by hairspray and make-up. Nowadays plastics are used more frequently in jewellery and once damaged they give off vapours that affect metals. Hence, the care of jewellery is complex.

Ancient jewellery should never be cleaned, nor painted pieces or very fragile pieces. A specialist conservator experienced in jewellery should perform this cleaning as they will not compromise condition or value. Ancient jewellery should only be repaired by a conservator or silversmith who is experienced in working with this type of material. Weak clasps and pins can be repaired, but if repairing historic pieces, make sure that the replacement is identical to the original. Loose stones should be repaired by a specialist because if they are not done properly, the repair may weaken the setting or damage the stone. Bead shops can provide information on restringing beads but if restringing is required for valuable, historic or precious beads and pearls, it is best done by a jeweller who is experienced in this service and will know the best methods.

You can clean slightly dull silver with a silver polishing cloth but if this does not work, consult a conservator. Likewise you can also clean jewellery containing precious stones, provided a piece is made from sound metal and the settings are open at the back. Gently use a soft brush dampened with detergent of conservation grade and warm water to remove loose dirt. Larger lumps of dirt may be removed by using a wooden tooth pick but never use metal implements. Also when you are cleaning jewellery, do so over a tray that can catch any pieces that may fall out. Rinse jewellery in warm water and dry with a soft cloth.

Ultrasonic cleaners are sometimes recommended for jewellery but these may be dangerous to use as precious stones may shatter if they are not properly used. It is wise to consult a specialist jeweller or conservator if you are in doubt.

When storing jewellery it is necessary to keep individual items of jewellery separate from each other. This is especially important with precious stones, such as diamonds, rubies, sapphires and emeralds, as gems can scratch other materials. Some gemstones (for example, emeralds) are brittle and they may become damaged if jumbled with other stones. Traditional jewellery cases, rolls and boxes are generally well designed and they will support jewellery items when they are not being worn.

Keep jewellery items of the same type or size together but not in contact with each other. For example, keep single-strand necklaces, bangles, earrings and brooches with similar pieces, and use acid-free tissue paper in boxes as a packing and cushioning material. Cotton wool should not be used as it may catch on jewellery items and it can cause corrosion if the air becomes damp. Also do not use coloured tissue paper with items made of pearl, ivory or bone because it can stain them. Silver items may be protected by good quality cotton cloth or a silver protection cloth.

Jewellery is generally kept at home, so there is always the risk of theft. For valuable pieces you have a better chance of recovery if you have a front and back photograph of a piece, as well as photographs of any special features such as engravings.

Conservation and restoration

The aim of conservation is to minimise the change to materials used in the making of collectables. In particular, conservation aims to protect collectables from the adverse effects of climate and chemical deterioration. Restoration entails treating collectables to enhance their interpretation; for example, inpainting losses in an oil painting so that the image's original appearance is maintained. Restoration may also involve the reassembly of displaced components, the removal of extraneous matter, or the integration of new materials or components to stabilise and strengthen the original artefact.

However, it is important to appreciate that an object may be worth more in the condition it has come to be in today than in its restored condition. For example, the *Titanic* sank in 1912 and let's say that a valuable ancient coin was recently recovered from the ship. Because it has been in the sea for 80 or more years it would appear damaged and corroded, but due to the history surrounding the *Titanic,* the coin may be worth more in its current condition than in its original condition. You would need to think very carefully before you restored such an item as there is a strong likelihood that the coin would be worth more in its corroded state. In its original condition, the coin would probably not be of interest to a museum or a one-off collector, but in its damaged condition it reflects the history of the *Titanic* and all that it entails and it would be extremely valuable.

If a collectable is damaged, a conservator can be productively employed to give an estimated cost for the required associated repairs. For example, if you are interested in buying a painting, you should request that the back be taken off and held up to the light. If the vendor will not take the back off, it may be because the paint is flaking off the canvas and if the painting was held up to the light, this would be revealed. If the paint is indeed flaking off, a conservator can give you an estimated cost for the necessary repairs.

When performing restoration work, conservators choose methods of 'minimal intervention', focusing on stabilisation and the retention of original material. Good conservators use materials with appropriate ageing characteristics and wherever possible use treatment methods that can be reversed. Conservators also document the condition of an item through written reports and photographs, both before and after treatment, in order to retain records of what has been changed for the benefit of future owners and caretakers.

Did you know ... Conservation of collectables is essential as damaged items are worth only a fraction of their value. Seek professional advice if you are in doubt.

Displaying collectables and interiors

The embellishments provided by collectables in a living space can dramatically set it apart from the ordinary. For those interested in collecting, collectables provide the icing on the cake when it comes to creating a home space, as it is the displays and decor that create the visual interest of a room. A home interior's unique personality and character can be defined by a grouping or scattering of images, photographs, antiques, paintings, prints, books, trinket boxes, jars, vases, pottery, porcelain and other items. For example, an arrangement on a tabletop of various collectables of different form and scale is interesting and immediately attracts a guest's interest. The first step in home decorating is to set essential room elements in place and the second step is to arrange items within rooms. There are limitless possibilities for utilising collectables in this process to brilliant effect.

Grouping

Valuable antiques and other collectables, such as paintings, prints and sculptures, can have a strong impact on the mood and style of a room's interior. As already discussed, collectables can provide touches of ingenuity and inspiration that add personality and character to a room. You will often find that grouping a collection of items together, rather than spreading them around your home, will generate the most impact. The same effect can be generated by grouping several eye-catching pieces together rather than positioning them individually. By presenting your collection well, an awkward-looking interior can be turned into a very pleasing, even stunning, space.

But decorating your home with collectables and generally beautiful items does not require perfection. Rather it requires creating an environment that reflects the inhabitant's personality and visual story of their life to date. You should begin with simplicity and seek to display striking and out-of-the ordinary items in groups or singly so that the effect is extraordinary. Smaller collectables such as jewellery—if you wish to display it—and items such as silver teaspoons need a dark background or a polished wooden tray to show them off. Grouping several collections of the same dominant idea creates a larger featured collection that can be the focal point of a room.

You should combine items that share the same colour, material, shape or motif. You can hang items such as commemorative mugs in an orderly fashion and complement this display with oversized mugs and cups and saucers in other parts of the room. A display of pieces such as blue and white china of different sizes and shapes complements larger pieces of oriental pottery and porcelain.

Did you know ...

Some collectables look attractive lined up in order of colour, height, pattern and shape while other items, such as large pieces of china and glass, warrant their own set of display shelves.

Display what is important to you

It is generally true that the collectables you choose to display reveal what is important to you, the householder, and in some instances may reveal a family history of many generations. Many collectables you own have a colourful history and represent a talking point in themselves.

It is recommended to select one or two large pieces as focal points, such as a painting or sculpture, but it is also feasible to select several smaller pieces with a common theme and group them together. Paintings or prints chosen in this manner can add life to an otherwise blank wall. If you collect photographs (signed ones are more valuable), they can make a fascinating feature on a wall, or individual ones lined up vertically can be hung between bookcases. You can show off family heirlooms, such as bangles, bracelets, necklaces and pendants, which may be pieces from long ago and therefore have historical significance.

Experiment

When done well, using collectables to enhance your decor adds personality and style to your home and reflects your creativity and ingenuity at the same time. Trying out your home-decorating ideas based around your collections is also a lot of fun. Collectables and accessories displayed in a room give clues and symbols of value, history, emotion and opinion. For example, a walnut grandfather clock embedded with mother of pearl is classic, functional and valuable, and symbolises accuracy, harmony and luxury. You can also use collectables, large or small, to suggest a powerful image. By blending forms, lines, motifs and textures with glass, gold and silver, tiny decorative embellishments and mirrors you will present your collectables cleverly and reflect prestige, and make your home stylishly cosy without suffocating it. A sincere and unique character can be conveyed through the use of bronze, clay, ivory, wood and ethnic fabrics.

Displaying collectables carefully

There are no hard and fast rules when it comes to displaying collectables and you might like to play around before you settle on particular layouts, but you must also be mindful about how an item will cope in its particular environment. For example, if you have a valuable rug, it is best to hang it on a wall where it will not be damaged. If you have a valuable painting, display it with a soft light that highlights it. Vases and glassware should be safely displayed in cabinets, and antiques should not be placed in main thoroughfares in your home. Always use common sense when displaying collectables as their value will be severely reduced if they become damaged.

Insurance

Taking care of collectables includes insuring them against loss or damage through fire, flood, theft and Acts of God. Your particular need for insurance may range from normal home and contents insurance if your collection is minor to having the highest coverage possible because your collectables are worth more than your property, and every contingency in between. Whatever the case, it is essential that you have adequate insurance to protect the value of your collectables. In deciding how best to insure your collectables you need to consider the following:

- Small-value items, such as one or two pieces of antique furniture, will not make any difference to your home and contents insurance premium.

- A large collection of art, antiques, heirlooms, coins, stamps, jewellery and so on will need special coverage insurance.

- Most home and contents insurance policies cover items valued at $2000 to $3000 but this can vary widely between insurance companies.

- While most home and contents policies cover personal property, you should read the policy carefully to ensure that all of your collectables are covered.

- If an item requires special coverage because its value is more than a few thousand dollars, you may need a valuation for insurance purposes.

- Calculate how much you have invested in collectables in your home in order to understand the importance of having special coverage.

- In most cases special coverage for collectables is not too expensive.

- Some insurance companies specialise in providing insurance for collectables.

- It is advisable to obtain insurance quotes from several insurance companies, especially if premiums seem too high.

- It is important to keep all invoices and receipts when purchasing collectables. These documents and a recent valuation are the security you will need if you have to make a claim.

- In view of the fact that you may one day need to make a claim, you should safely store photographs of items for which you are seeking special coverage.

- Collectors need insurance that will cover the full value of their items as well as the individual parts in case individual items are stolen or damaged, so keep your insurance company up to date on any new additions.

Did you know ... Collectables may be old, so you need to be sure that your insurance company will replace an item if lost or stolen, or give you a monetary equivalent.

Insurance policies often specify 'new for old' replacement, which is inappropriate for collectables. Make sure that your policy covers exactly what you have in mind.

Before you travel, check your insurance policy to see if it covers items that you acquire while you are away, as some insurance companies may not provide cover until you return home.

Regular valuation

Be careful not to under-insure your collectables. Since they will appreciate over time, you need up-to-date valuations. Most collectables do not generate an income stream, so their value to you is tied up in capital appreciation. You should periodically have your collectables revalued to take into account price increases or else you risk making a substantial loss in the event of fire or theft.

Inventory

It is important to make an inventory of your collectables, which may just be a list of everything you own. Each item on the list should then have its value assessed. This will give you a good idea of what needs to be insured, as well as provide a total value for your collectables. Professional valuers do this when they construct a depreciation schedule for a client. To obtain item values, have cost prices and possible capital appreciation since you bought an item assessed. For major items it is also wise to get a valuation for insurance purposes, although bear in mind that the insurance value could be very different from the price you obtain when you sell the items.

Key points

- All materials deteriorate naturally over time and it is not possible to prevent this; however, the pace of deterioration can be reduced through proper care and treatment.

- Light, temperature and humidity can damage collectables but these factors can all be controlled.

- The proper care of many collectables entails minimum physical handling.

- Jewellery is just one type of collectable that requires special care. Most damage to jewellery arises through wear and tear, and very old jewellery should never be worn.

- If you are in doubt about any aspect of care of a collectable, consult a conservator. Note that due to historical significance a collectable may be worth more unrestored than in its original condition.

- When it comes to displaying collectables, there are no hard and fast rules, but you will need to be mindful of conditions that will minimise their deterioration.

- If exhibited appropriately, collectables can be the focal point of a room.

- It is always advisable to insure collectables. Sometimes normal home and contents insurance will cover a collectable, while in other cases you will need to take out special coverage.

- Make sure that your insurance policy covers 'old for old' replacement of collectables and not 'new for old' replacement.

5

The legal framework and collectables

The impact of legislation on investing in collectables can be seen in a number of areas. For a start, if you invest in collectables as a business, you will be liable to pay income tax on your profits. Collectables are also eligible investments for self managed superannuation funds (SMSFs), subject to compliance with a number of rules. Collectables are specifically included in capital gains tax (CGT) legislation. Other legislation, such as the *Protection of Movable Cultural Heritage Act 1986*, has prompted the adoption of a national Indigenous Australian Art Commercial Code of Conduct. The *Resale Royalty Right for Visual Artists Act 2009* is another piece of legislation that can affect investments in collectables. Finally, some people like to leave bequests of collectables in their wills, which may have tax implications for the beneficiaries.

Income tax

For most people, collecting is a hobby and on this basis any profit made is not subject to income tax. However, if you are in the business of collecting, the proceeds from sales are included in your assessable income. You can then claim your expenses as tax deductions. You pay tax on your assessable income minus your allowable deductions according to your income tax bracket. The ATO, <www.ato.gov.au>, has issued guidelines as to what constitutes operating a business, as seen in the following list.*

- Does your activity have a significant commercial character? It is important to consider whether you carry on your activity for commercial reasons and in a commercially viable manner.

- Do you have more than just an intention to engage in business? You must have made a decision to start your business and have done something about it. If you are still setting up or preparing to go into business, you might not yet have started the business.

- Do you have the purpose of profit as well as the prospect of profit? Do you intend to make a profit or genuinely believe you will make a profit, even if you are unlikely to do so in the short-term?

- Is there repetition and regularity to your activity? Businesses usually repeat similar types of activities, although one-off transactions can constitute a business in some cases.

- Is your business similar to other businesses in your industry? Is the way you operate consistent with industry norms or other businesses in your industry?

- What is the size, scale or permanency of your activity? Is the size or scale of your activity consistent with other businesses in your industry? Is it sufficient to allow you to make a sustainable profit?

- Is your activity planned, organised and carried out in a business-like manner? This can be shown using business and accounting records, a separate business bank account, business premises, licences or qualifications, and a registered business name.

The issues discussed indicate the factors that courts and tribunals take into account when assessing whether a business exists for tax purposes. The ATO says that while no one factor can be used to work out whether you are carrying out a business, taken together they can show whether your activity is classified as a business.

---

* From 'Tax Basics For Small Business', p. 6, ATO, 2010, copyright Commonwealth of Australia, reproduced by permission.

As you can see from the guidelines, most collectors fall within the hobbyist category and are therefore engaged in recreational pursuits, but you can be deemed to be operating a business with just one transaction if you fall within other parameters and in that case the income derived from collectables is subject to income tax.

Did you know ...

The advantage of being classed as a hobbyist is that the only tax you pay is on capital gains and then only if an item costs more than $500.

Negative gearing art rentals

Negative gearing is most commonly associated with investment properties but it can be used with any asset that has the potential to appreciate in value. Negative gearing occurs when you borrow money to buy an asset and the income that is generated is less than your interest payments and other outgoings. In other words, you are making a running loss on your investment. As any loss made through negative gearing can be offset against your other income—for example, your salary—you are generating a tax deduction from your investment.

If you are on the highest marginal tax rate of 45 per cent, the government subsidises nearly half your loss. The advantage to you is that you get the use of someone else's money at a rate subsidised by the government to finance an asset that you expect will appreciate in value. Of course, there is a risk that if the asset does not appreciate sufficiently in value, your plans would not come to fruition and you would still make a loss—even after taking into account the tax deductions.

Negative gearing can be profitably employed in conjunction with art rentals. This can best be illustrated with an example.

Say you bought a painting by Adam Cullen for $15 000 with an interest only loan of $12 400. Following is a summary of the details:

- acquisition cost—$15 000

- valuation fee—$150

- framing/stretching fee — $250

- total consideration — $15 400

- yearly outgoings — $240 (portfolio management fee, insurance, etc.)

- interest rate on loan — 10.99 per cent per annum (secured personal loan)

- loan amount — $12 400

- yearly interest repayments — $1363 (rounded)

- rental term — three years

- rental yield — 8 per cent per annum (guaranteed)

- yearly income — $1200

- capital appreciation — 10 per cent per annum (estimate)

- sale price at end of rental — $19 965

- marginal rate of tax — 45 per cent.

A year-by-year analysis of this scenario is shown in table 5.1. Effectively you make an investment of $3000 at the beginning of Year 1, make a small net loss after tax of $216 in Years 1 and 2, and receive cash in Year 3 of $6287. The rate of return from this investment is 23.8 per cent per annum, which is far better than the 8 per cent per annum yield you would have achieved if you had not negatively geared your investment. The indicative interest rate of 10.99 per cent used in this example is high by some standards and you could probably do better than this, which would serve to boost your return even further. You are also foregoing income on the $3000 for three years — say at 6 per cent per annum — so you need to deduct another $180 per year ($540 in total) minus tax in compound interest.

Using this analysis you can then ask a series of 'What if?' questions. For example, what would your return be if the painting appreciated by only 5 per cent per annum instead of 10 per cent per annum? The sale price would be $17 365 and the return would be 8.25 per cent per annum, which is about the same as the yield ungeared. However, you would be much better off if the painting appreciated by more than 5 per cent per annum, which is a modest target for a mid-career artist in today's market.

Table 5.1: year-by-year analysis

	Year 0 ($)	Year 1 ($)	Year 2 ($)	Year 3 ($)
Total outlay	(15 400)	–	–	–
Loan	12 400			
Yearly income		1200	1200	1200
Yearly outgoings		(240)	(240)	(240)
Interest*		(1363)	(1363)	(1363)
Net loss		(403)	(403)	(403)
Tax benefit @ 46.5%		187	187	187
After tax loss		(216)	(216)	(216)
Sale price				19 965
Loan repayment				(12 400)
Capital gains tax				(1062)
Cash flow	(3000)	(216)	(216)	6287

* Annual interest = $12 400 × 10.99% = $1362.76 = $1363 rounded.

Following is a summary of the CGT calculation:

Sale price	$19 965
Purchase price	$15 400
Capital gain	$4565
Discount (50%)	$2282.50 (Held for more than 12 months)
Net capital gain	$2282.50
Tax @ 46.5%	$1061.36
Rounded	$1062

When the rental term expires at the end of three years you could seek to arrange another three-year rental on the same terms and continue to earn 23.8 per cent per annum (assuming the same conditions). There is no guarantee you will be able to do this, but it is another option available to you. A further option is to keep the painting for your own enjoyment, but you would need to renegotiate the loan (or pay it off) and you would be out of pocket $1363 a year in interest charges. You could not, however, continue to negatively gear the investment because it does not generate an income.

Sometimes the ATO will not allow you to negatively gear an investment—for example, insurance and friendly society bonds—so you should seek a product ruling before you endeavour to negatively gear in the art-rental market.

Did you know ... The chief disadvantage with negative gearing is that the underlying asset does not appreciate in value to the extent you would like.

Capital gains tax

Specific sections of the Income Tax Act relate to collectables. Section 108–10(2) says that a collectable means any of the following assets that are kept mainly for the personal use and enjoyment of a taxpayer or his or her associates:

- artwork, jewellery, an antique or coin or medallion

- a rare folio, manuscript or book

- a postage stamp or first day cover.

A collectable is also deemed to include an interest in any of these assets, a debt arising from any of these assets or an option or right to acquire any of these assets. The ATO considers that an antique is any object of artistic and historical significance that is at least 100 years old at the time of its disposal.

If a collectable is acquired for $500 or less, any gain or loss for capital gains tax (CGT) purposes is ignored. It should be noted that any goods and services tax (GST) input tax credits are ignored for the purpose of this threshold test. Where a collectable is acquired for more than $500, CGT is payable on any profit made on disposal. If you have held a collectable for more than 12 months, you can claim a 50 per cent discount on the amount of the capital gain.

Capital losses from the disposal of collectables (that have been acquired for more than $500) can be offset against the capital gains from collectables but not against capital gains from any other assets, such as shares, or against other income, such as salary or interest received. If a capital loss from a collectable in an income year exceeds capital gains from collectables, then the excess is carried forward to be applied in the order in which the losses were made. Capital losses from the disposal of other assets can be offset against the net capital gains from collectables.

> **Did you know ...**
>
> Capital gains tax is not payable on any asset acquired prior to 20 September 1985. If purchased after this date, you are liable to CGT but it may be calculated under different bases. If held longer than 12 months, you can claim a 50 per cent discount.

Note that the definition of 'collectables' does not include motor vehicles, which are included as 'personal use assets'. Where a personal use asset is acquired for $10 000 or less, any gain made on a subsequent disposal is exempt from CGT. But as most motor vehicles depreciate rather than appreciate, it is unlikely that you would ever pay CGT on the family car anyway. Capital losses from the sale of a personal use asset such as a motor vehicle are never allowable for CGT purposes. The reason for this is that allowing such losses would result in the ATO losing too much revenue as most motor vehicles are sold at a loss.

Jointly held assets

Where you own a collectable jointly with others, other than a debt, option or right, the $500 threshold applies to the market value of the underlying collectable at the time you acquired your interest. This means that if, for example, a rare coin had a market value of $2000 and you acquired a 10 per cent share in it — that is, $200 worth — you would be subject to CGT on disposal of the coin because the underlying value of the coin exceeded the $500 threshold even though your share was only $200. This is to prevent a group of people getting together and buying a number of collectables with individual shares of less than $500 and therefore not being subject to CGT.

Self managed superannuation funds

A self managed superannuation fund (SMSF) is a do-it-yourself superannuation fund where you take responsibility for managing your own retirement funds. The main advantages of having an SMSF are that you maximise the tax benefits of superannuation while retaining control of your investments. Provided your fund has fewer than five members, it will be classified as an 'excluded' fund and it will be exempt from the more onerous regulations that apply to larger funds. Usually in an excluded fund all members are also trustees of the fund. Being a trustee of your own SMSF means that you have absolute control over where the fund invests its money, providing these investments are in accordance with the fund's trust deed and superannuation regulations. But you also have many legal obligations and responsibilities as a trustee of the fund.

The earnings of superannuation funds are taxed at 15 per cent compared with the top personal rate of tax of 46.5 per cent (including the Medicare levy). CGT is payable by superannuation funds at 15 per cent but there is a discount of one-third on assets held for more than 12 months (compared with a 50 per cent discount for individuals), so the equivalent CGT rate is 10 per cent (two-thirds × 15 per cent). The main disadvantages of SMSFs are the time it takes to manage the fund and the administrative cost. For example, it is not generally worthwhile to set up an SMSF with less than $120000 or if you don't think that there will be more than $120000 in the fund in the near future.

Collectables and SMSFs

Notwithstanding that the Cooper Review recommended that art and other collectables not be allowed as SMSF investments, the federal government has confirmed, subject to certain limitations, that an SMSF can hold collectables in its portfolio of assets. In fact, the arts industry has become reliant on the investment of SMSFs, and Lowenstein Arts Management estimates that it now accounts for around 15 per cent of turnover. It adds that for Aboriginal art this figure could be higher. The fact is that no-one knows for sure how much is held in collectables in SMSFs, although at the time of writing the Cooper Panel estimated it at $500 million.

Did you know … The eligibility of collectables as SMSF assets was under threat early in 2010, but the federal government has confirmed that they are acceptable.

There are two overriding requirements for collectables to be considered eligible investments—strategy and the sole purpose test.

SMSF investment strategy

Firstly, there needs to be an investment strategy developed by the trustees that provides for investment in collectables. This document needs to be based on sound business principles and it needs to make a case as to why investment in collectables is desirable. The sort of areas an investment strategy needs to cover includes:

- growth
- risk
- liquidity
- return
- diversity.

SMSFs are primarily governed by the provisions of the *Superannuation Industry (Supervision) Act 1993*. Some important sections include:

- Section 52(2) (f), which requires trustees to formulate and give effect to an investment strategy that has regard to the whole circumstances of the fund including risk, diversification, liquidity and solvency.

- Section 62, which essentially requires that the sole purpose of the fund be the provision of retirement benefits and/or death benefits.

- Section 66, which says that subject to certain exceptions the trustee is prohibited from intentionally acquiring assets from related parties of the fund.

- Section 109, which requires the trustee to operate on commercial terms.

In pursuing their investment strategy trustees would be ill-advised to buy collectables at a street stall or flea market but if they relied on the expert advice of a consultant or dealer and made purchases through more conventional channels, their investment strategy is more likely to meet the necessary requirements.

SMSF sole purpose test

The second prerequisite for including collectables in SMSFs is that they satisfy the sole purpose test. This test effectively stipulates that the exclusive purpose of superannuation is to fund retirement. There are a limited number of other purposes that are allowed, such as providing for total and permanent disability, but the enjoyment that comes from looking at art and other collectables is not included. The Administrative Appeals Tribunal has shown in decisions that it will consider whether a trustee has a secondary purpose in making assets available for their own use or the use of family or friends when determining whether an investment breaches the sole purpose test.

SMSFs and displaying assets

An investment strategy has as its aim the use of an SMSF's assets to achieve a desired goal and a minimum level of performance. It is a plan for investing, maintaining and realising the fund's assets in terms of the overall objective of the fund. It does not matter that most collectables do not generate an income stream because many assets—for example, some shares, land and so on—are held for their potential for capital appreciation. However, it is in the storing of collectables and possible breaches of the sole purpose test that you may come unstuck. In the event you store artwork, for example, on your wall at home, you may be deemed to be deriving personal use or enjoyment from it. Storing artwork on a wall is not a problem, but deriving personal use or enjoyment from looking at it is. To avoid any doubt, you may need to put collectables into storage or lend them to an art gallery in return for the gallery providing storage by hanging it on its wall.

If your SMSF owns collectables, the safest thing to do to meet the sole purpose test is to put them into storage.

SMSFs and renting out assets

It is possible for an SMSF to buy a collectable from an arm's length third party and lease it at a market rate of rent to a member of the SMSF. This is most commonly done with art but it could apply to any collectable. Factors to look out for include:

- The fund's investment strategy needs to incorporate investing in collectables.

- The trustee needs knowledge and some expertise in dealing in collectables, and should seek expert advice on the soundness of investments.

- The member who leases the collectable needs to pay a market rate of rent. This should be verified by someone other than the trustee.

- The SMSF must be no worse off than if it leased the collectable to someone else.

- It is the purpose of providing the benefit—that is, monetary gain—that determines whether the sole purpose test is met.

- The lease must be subject to normal commercial conditions and controls.

- The member to whom the collectable is leased can use it for his or her own personal enjoyment but the trustee needs to be sure they will take care of it.

Note that according to what are referred to as the 'in-house' rules it is permissible for a member of an SMSF to hold 5 per cent of the net market value of an SMSF in the form of artworks at their home. However, it is recommended that even in this case the SMSF receive a rental payment from the member for the enjoyment of the artwork.

Trustees always need to be able to demonstrate that they have taken adequate precautions to protect any collectable held by a fund. The collectable should be kept in a secure location and it should be stored in such a way as to minimise damage. Collectables must be adequately insured by the fund. All procedures need to be properly minuted.

Detailed expert advice should be sought if a collectable is held for purposes of capital appreciation, as opposed to deriving an income stream. Documentation should be prepared and kept regarding annual costs, such as insurance, storage and valuation costs.

Wine and SMSFs

You need to seek expert advice if you are investing in wine within an SMSF structure as this is a difficult area. As discussed in chapter 2, one of the things you need to do if you collect wine is to monitor the progress of your cellar from time to time by drinking an occasional bottle. On the surface this breaches the sole purpose test, so you may need to arrange an arm's length transaction whereby someone else monitors your cellar for a fee, but this can detract from being a wine collector in the first place. If you wish to try the wine yourself, you would have to buy a bottle from your collection at the market rate.

Fascinating collectables ...

Car number plates

Collecting car number plates is a popular pastime in the US. In Australia the practice is less widespread, although still prevalent. The most valuable number plates are low-digit plates that carry with them 'right to display', which means you have the right to put them on your car. The record price paid at auction for a low-digit number plate was $680 000 in 2003 for 'NSW 2'. Rumour has it that 'NSW 6' changed hands after an auction a few years later for as much as $1 million. The record price for a two-digit plate, 'NSW 18', is $248 600. In Victoria a record price was set for a three-digit plate when 'Victoria 626' sold for $24 860. Low-digit NSW number plates tend to sell for much more than Victorian ones.

Other low-digit number plates may have added value because the numbers correspond with the model of an expensive car. For example, it has been suggested that the owner of a Ferrari 599 GTB Fiorano purchased number plate '599' for $94 000 in August 2010. Another significant Ferrari plate, '412', sold for $65 000.

Outside the low-digit number plate range, other number plates are much less expensive and are also suitable for investment. For example, you could collect a series of number plates beginning with every letter of the alphabet for $10 to $1000 per plate. Limited edition number plates are worth more; for example, number plates produced for official vehicles at the 1956 Melbourne Olympics, which sell today for $2000 to $3000. Similar number plates are available for the Perth Commonwealth Games in 1962 (worth about $1200) and the 1982 Brisbane Commonwealth Games (worth about $200).

Did you know ... Do not serve members of your SMSF wine at a dinner party unless you have bought it for market price as part of an arm's length transaction

The *Protection of Movable Cultural Heritage Act 1986* (Commonwealth)

The *Protection of Movable Cultural Heritage Act 1986* (PMCH Act) was designed to prevent the permanent export of culturally significant material. The PMCH Act had as its foundation a balance between the property rights of owners and the national interest. Under the terms of this Act, anyone who wishes to export an item on the Control List of prohibited exports has to apply to the federal government for a permit. Specified objects covered by the PMCH Act include fossils, meteorites, minerals, agricultural and industrial heritage, and so on, but for the purposes of this book notable objects include:

- Indigenous art and artefacts

- works of fine and decorative art

- books, stamps and medals

- historic materials.

The PMCH Act was amended in 1998 to reflect market-value changes and to effectively bring all the formative paintings from the birth of the modern Indigenous movement at Papunya Tula in the 1970s within the ambit of the Act. Between 2003 and 2007 nearly 600 export applications were made under the Act and almost all in the fine art categories were by auction houses in relation to Aboriginal art.

The intention of the PMCH Act when it was introduced was that if a work was denied an export permit, it would be acquired by an institution, or in the case of Aboriginal material it would be returned to the community. Despite this, there were early warnings that the Act would adversely affect the market, especially for Aboriginal art. According to Sotheby's, a large number of high-end sales to foreign collectors have been thwarted and there has been a significant drop in pre-sale interest. Under the Act a National Cultural Heritage Fund was established to foster acquisition of these artworks in Australia but so far only one Papunya Tula work has been bought using the fund's resources. On the other hand, in the two-year period of 2001–03 alone a total of 10 Papunya Tula works were denied export permits. Hence the scheme is not working as planned.

The PMCH Act is under review by the government. Submissions made include some notable ones that would allow the Minister for the Arts to declare exports outside existing date limits prohibited in some cases. This potential provision is specifically aimed at Aboriginal art where some paintings were done by elders in spurts at irregular intervals; however, the effect would be to make it possible for any major work of art to be potentially denied export.

The federal government may also look to other countries for ideas within its review. For example, in the UK legislation requires that if a work is denied an export permit, it must be purchased by someone else; for example, a government-sponsored fund. This ensures that there is a market for artwork denied access to export markets by law.

The implication of this Act for investors is that you may be sold a collectable that cannot be exported, which means that if you wish to on-sell an item, the market will be limited to Australia. For many collectables this will not matter, but for something such as Indigenous art it could have a negative impact on its future value. Be sure if you are buying such artwork that there is no prohibition on export.

Did you know ...

The PMCH Act was introduced to safeguard Australia's national interests but it has had an adverse affect on investment markets.

The *Resale Royalty Right for Visual Artists Act 2009* (Commonwealth)

The *Resale Royalty Right for Visual Artists Act 2009* came into effect on 9 June 2010. All artists benefit, but the intent of the legislation was to particularly help Indigenous artists. However, there are numerous critics who believe it will harm the Aboriginal art industry because it necessitates costly administration and causes confusion among buyers.

The scheme entitles artists to a 5 per cent royalty on the commercial resale of designated works of art that cost $1000 or more. Artworks covered include:

- paintings

- drawings

- sculpture

- ceramics

- glassware

- tapestries

- photographs

- weavings

- fine art jewellery.

Limited edition prints, photographs and sculptures, provided they are authorised by the artist, are also included, as are newer artworks such as installations, digital artworks and multimedia artworks. Manuscripts are excluded as are mass-produced items such as posters. The scheme applies for 70 years after an artist's death.

Royalties are payable on resale of an artwork, except for the first sale after 8 June 2010 even if that is a resale. Hence royalties are initially expected to be small. The scheme Act is administered by Copyright Agency Ltd (CAL), which the government has appointed for five years from April 2010. Since June 2010, buyers, sellers, auction houses, galleries and dealers have been legally obliged to provide information to CAL about all commercial resales, including those that do not generate royalties. CAL believes that the information collected this way will be useful for a range of purposes, including determining provenance.

The scheme applies only to artworks resold in Australia, and not if they are sold by someone overseas to another person overseas. However, it is unlikely that this will change because of the practical difficulties involved in administering a scheme overseas. The federal government is providing $1.5 million over three years to administer the scheme, a significant part of which has been allocated to an education program for artists and the art trade.

Those who criticise the scheme point to the extra administration required by auction houses, dealers, galleries and so on, and also say that it does not benefit the artists who need financial aid the most. They also believe that only living artists should benefit and the structure of the current scheme will benefit the descendants of artists such as Brett Whiteley and Fred Williams, who already do well in the primary market. It is noted that a similar scheme operates in France and the bulk of resale royalties flow to the estates of only a handful of artists.

The impact of this legislation on investors is yet to be determined, but it is likely that the cost of the royalty will eventually be passed on to buyers by dealers and auction houses. Generally speaking the Act does not apply to the first sale after it took effect, but the legislation's impact is to introduce price uncertainty into the market.

Leaving collectables in your will

If a collector intends to keep their collectables until they die, they can leave bequests in their will to designated beneficiaries. Remember that with some collectables—for example, stamps—a complete series is generally worth more than the sum of the individual parts that make up the series. Hence, a collector should think carefully before breaking up a set. A collector should also make sure that the description of what they are bequeathing is unmistakable and easily located because they will not be around to sort out any confusion. For example, if you are bequeathing an ancient coin, you should describe where it can be found and the container that houses it, as well as the coin itself.

Did you know …

Planning for what will happen to your collection when you die is an important consideration in investment collecting. If left to the wrong person, all your good work could be undone.

Capital gains tax on inheritances

After a lifetime of collecting, people sometimes leave bequests of whole collections to institutions such as museums and art galleries. Often these are not appreciated as much as might be expected because of the costs involved in maintaining the collection. Much will depend on the significance of the collection, so you should approach the institution before you die and sort it out then. If you leave your pieces to a not-for-profit organisation, there are no CGT implications.

If you leave your collectables to individuals, the repercussions from a CGT point of view will vary depending upon when you acquired the collectables. If you acquired a piece prior to 20 September 1985 and bequeath it to a friend or relative after that date, the beneficiary will be deemed to have acquired it at the date of your death for its market value. Then when they sell it, they will be liable for CGT at their marginal rate of tax on the difference between the selling price and the market value at the time of your death subject to a 50 per cent discount. Note that if it is a collectable that appreciates significantly in value after death, it could push the beneficiary into a higher tax bracket, so CGT could be substantial when they come to sell it years later.

If a collectable was purchased on or after 20 September 1985, a beneficiary is deemed to have acquired it at the date of your death for asset's cost base, indexed cost base or reduced cost base, whichever is relevant according to choices you can make under income tax law. It is best to contact the ATO if you are in this situation, but basically it is the collectable's cost price adjusted for inflation. Hypothetically, a collectable that was bought in 1986 could be inherited much later, so there could be a good deal of capital appreciation. If the beneficiary wishes to sell it straight away, they could be hit with a hefty CGT bill. Again CGT is payable at the beneficiary's marginal rate of tax and a 50 per cent discount applies notwithstanding that there may be less than 12 months between when the beneficiary inherited the asset and when they sold it. The important date for determining the 50 per cent discount is the date that the deceased acquired the collectable, not when the beneficiary inherited it.

Key points

- For most people collecting is a hobby rather than a profit-making enterprise, so collectors are not generally subject to income tax. However, a one-off transaction can constitute a business in some circumstances.

- You can substantially boost the returns you can earn from art rentals through negative gearing.

- Specific sections of the Income Tax Act relate to collectables. Where a collectable is acquired for more than $500, CGT is payable on any profit made on disposal.

- Collectables are eligible investments for SMSFs but this is subject to strict rules.

- An SMSF needs a collectables investment strategy that covers growth, risk, liquidity, return and diversity.

- The sole purpose test requires that SMSFs focus exclusively on providing retirement benefits.

- The *Protection of Movable Cultural Heritage Act 1986* denies the export of some collectables.

- The *Resale Royalty Right for Visual Artists Act 2009* may serve to increase prices for artworks in secondary markets.

- There can be CGT consequences when leaving collectables in your will.

6

Buying and selling through dealers and privately

Being an investor and a collector is often viewed as a contradiction in terms. The part of you that is an investor is looking for items that will appreciate in price, while the collector in you wants prices to remain low so that you can buy more of them. The investor in you looks for opportunities to sell items at a good price, while the collector in you does not want to reduce your collection. The conundrum is always with you as you engage in your hobby and seek to make a profit from it at the same time.

This chapter looks at buying and selling collectables with the emphasis on private purchases and sales, and trading with dealers. (Chapter 7 discusses buying and selling at auction.) The golden rule is to buy and sell what you genuinely find to be enjoyable. If you do not feel comfortable with an item, do not buy it in the first place, regardless of its investment potential because collectables are meant to be kept for the long-term and you will have to live with them. This book is not written for speculators.

To succeed in investing in collectables you will need to both buy astutely and sell when prices are on the boil. In the sharemarket this is called 'buying in gloom and selling in boom'. The first rule of buying is to purchase the best items you can afford. You may have to wait longer to save the necessary money, or you may have to settle for a smaller item, but always buy quality over quantity. The main reason is that you will find the collectable easier to sell, both in good markets and bad. Also, as well as retaining their value better in bad markets, good quality collectables tend to appreciate in value faster than lesser quality items.

Private trading

To make money from private trading you need to beat dealers at their own game. A prerequisite for this is to become an expert in your field of collecting. An expert investment collector undertakes a lifetime of serious study of their chosen field of specialisation because this enables them to gain an edge in finding undervalued items. Becoming an expert requires considerable dedication, time, love and study of your subject area. The 'expert' route to successful investment collecting is one of the best and least dangerous ways to making profits, always assuming that you do indeed qualify for the title.

Before you buy or sell anything it is essential that you develop as much knowledge of your specialist area as possible.

Buying and selling through private trading

When you are ready to buy, do what dealers do and place an advertisement in a newspaper announcing that you are interested in buying a certain type of item. It could be any type of collectable but let's say that you specialise in Australian pennies. You may have to do house calls, or encourage interested sellers to come to you. Real bargains can be obtained by buying multi-coin collections rather than individual items, so be prepared for sellers with bags and books of pennies. Of course, you will need to have built up your knowledge of pennies to be able to assess collections and strike a profitable deal. You may come across sellers who have no idea of the value of what they are selling. This is where your homework is important.

Private trading is time-consuming. You need to place advertisements and often meet with buyers and sellers personally. When trading with dealers you just go into their shop and do business.

Whatever your speciality, 'for sale' advertisements in newspapers can signify a bargain, providing they are not placed by dealers. The reason is that the selling prices do not reflect a dealer's mark-up, which varies but is usually between 33 and 50 per cent, although it can be more. You can also visit junk shops and local markets. Unlike fully fledged dealers, stall holders pay lower overheads than dealers with an established business in a gallery or shop, so you may find a bargain at a market. However, there is a higher likelihood that you will come across fakes and frauds in this scenario, so be on your guard.

When you are looking for items to buy keep in mind that a series or set of items will be worth more than the sum of the items alone. Some investment collectors only acquire series or sets. They collect them in the hope that the sum will be more valuable than the total of the parts individually. On a simple level, two matching candlesticks will be more valuable together than singly. Likewise a complete set of an artist's prints will be worth more than the prints on their own. As a rule of thumb, you should not seek to break a series or set if you have the opportunity to buy it complete and, if you are selling complete, do not break it up and sell the items individually. Another useful rule of thumb is that the larger the series or set of items, the more valuable it will be in proportion to the value of one item—that is, there is an exponential relationship. For example, four candlesticks might be worth five times the value of one singly but six candlesticks might be worth 10 times the value of one on its own.

Private trading advantages and disadvantages

Dealing privately with individuals can be profitable but it can also be time-consuming and even at the end of negotiations you still may not have a sale. You have to balance the prospect of getting a better price against these potential disadvantages. Bear in mind that there are no mark-ups or commissions when you deal privately, but most people at some time have had the experience of dealing with a 'ratbag'.

If you buy a collectable privately, you most probably will have no chance of returning it later if you are not happy with your purchase. If it is a case of fraud, you will have legal redress but this is an unenviable situation to be in and it is best avoided in the first place. Caveat emptor, or 'let the buyer beware', applies very much in the case of private sales. There is an obvious increased likelihood of being sold a fake and you should call in an expert if you are in doubt. If you are buying a work of art or piece of sporting memorabilia, ask for a certificate of authenticity, but be prepared for the strong possibility that none exists.

Did you know ...

Some people enjoy the personal contact that comes with private trading while others do not like the hassles. It is much like buying and selling second-hand cars privately as opposed to doing business with a dealer or just trading it in.

Unlike operating with a dealer with whom you have a good relationship, there is no prospect of taking an item home and seeing if it 'fits' with your decor before you make up your mind to buy it. You are the new owner when the deal is struck. On the other hand, you have the benefit of being able to negotiate face-to-face with the seller when you buy privately, whereas dealers' prices are usually fixed.

Another advantage of buying privately is that there is a greater likelihood of discovering the provenance of an item, which is its chain of ownership. You may also stand a better chance of learning who owned an item before the current owner if you buy privately. Perhaps it is a family heirloom, which would add interest to your purchase. Or you may be told a plausible lie ...

By buying and selling privately you eliminate the middlemen from the process. There is no mark-up, commission or other fees to pay. A dealers' mark-up can be more than 50 per cent, and auction houses charge commission on both buying and selling as well as other incidental charges, such as photography.

Associations and trade fairs

Member associations will often help you build a collection for better prices than if you purchase on the open market. For example, stamps, comic books, car parts and coins may all be purchased through regional clubs or associations at lower prices than on the open market and with an accurate assessment of the item on offer. Because of their mutual interest, association members may be open to barter and trade, and a serious collector would benefit by joining such an association.

Trade fairs, for example, antique and record fairs, have become increasingly popular and a knowledgeable buyer can do well at these events. The vendors know the value of what they are selling, however, and their prices will reflect this. To be safe, ensure that you are buying from members of the trade association and that you receive the same guarantee as if you were making your purchase at a regular retail outlet.

Dealers

An alternative to private trading is to build up associations with dealers whose job it is to service collectors. However, at the outset note that as an investment collector you buy particular pieces that in the future may be worth far more than present prices. It is also essential to appreciate that fashions change and what may be in demand at one time may be out of favour at another. For example, in antique furniture, Victoriana was once highly in demand, but then high quality 20th-century retro became the fashion. Similarly, in the field of rugs, tribal rugs not made for the commercial market became more collectable than Oriental rugs. These types of trends may compromise the advice that a dealer gives you.

Although dealers are well positioned to identify these trends at an early stage and advise you accordingly, they are also in business for themselves and seek any business they will push their own wares. So you may be encouraged to buy collectables that are on their way out of fashion (or at least you may not be discouraged from buying them). This potential problem can be mitigated by consulting with several dealers and keeping an open mind in terms of what they tell you. As will be discussed in this chapter, a good dealer-client relationship is invaluable, but you should also keep your own knowledge up to date so that you can have educated discussions with dealers.

Buying through dealers

A relationship with a dealer comes about through making purchases over a period of time. Dealers are goldmines of information, which they will happily share with you as long as you remain an active client. A dealer will be reluctant to share too much of their knowledge with those who do not have a genuine purchasing history. Subject to the proviso that dealers are in business and have to make a living by selling collectables, their advice is invaluable.

Did you know ...

If you are making a one-off purchase, any dealer who has what you want at the price you're willing to pay will suffice.

Once you decide to specialise in an area—Arthur Boyd prints, for example—you can expect your dealer to contact you when one comes up. It is likely that you will receive advance information on what has become available and you might even get a discount of 10 per cent to 20 per cent for a prompt sale. A good dealer will also reimburse any purchase with which you are not satisfied. You have the dealer's guarantee against fakes, although a dealer's guarantee is only as good as the dealer's reputation.

Tell the dealer about what you like and do not like and why you are interested in buying. It is a good idea to not tell a dealer that you are buying for investment purposes because they will probably not react positively. However, dealers are aware that their clients have an eye for capital appreciation, so it would not be a total surprise. Also tell the dealer what your limits are. They will keep you informed of what they have bought as well as items coming up for sale, and they will also act for you at purchasing time. For this service the dealer will probably charge you around 10 per cent of the purchase price, which will be well worth it.

When buying from a dealer, the price is generally fixed. There may be a small discount for cash or for some other reason, but do not expect to wheel and deal or treat their business like a bazaar. A dealer's price is a considered price, partly based on market demand and partly determined by what the dealer paid for an item. All dealers have current trade price lists. No prices are ever pulled out of the air.

If you are concentrating on a particular area, finding a dealer and then getting to know and trust them is similar to relying on a good financial adviser. It will cost you money, but it is worth it. Like any profession, there are good and bad dealers, so build your relationship gradually. Naturally they are in business to make a profit like anyone else in private enterprise. A good dealer may let you know when they encounter a collectable of the sort you are interested in and, for a small fee, bid on your behalf at auctions. Also, when considering buying furniture and paintings, if an item will have an impact on your surroundings, a dealer may lend you a piece to see how it 'fits' before you buy it. A dealer may do this even if you are not a regular client, but then they will charge a small fee. This service can save you considerable disappointment.

You may get an opportunity to buy from a printed or online catalogue without viewing an item. However, it is essential if at all possible to view any items before you buy or to consult with an authority that can assess damage and condition. Catalogue sales usually carry the same guarantee as retail purchases. Successful dealers and collectors file and cross-reference catalogues and keep them indefinitely, so you should always keep catalogues.

Did you know ...

A dealer's stock is constantly turning over so make regular visits to those you prefer. But bear in mind that you will outstay your welcome if you never buy anything.

Selling through dealers

If you have built up your collection with purchases from one main dealer, you might make this dealer your first port of call. Sometimes a dealer will offer to buy your total collection back from you. If that is the case, you will have to work out a price. The dealer will probably ask you directly how much you want for the collection. However, it is far better if the dealer makes you an offer, so ensure that they do this. If the amount is in the vicinity of what you are looking for, add 10 per cent in your mind and negotiate from there. For example, the dealer might offer you $50 000. You could then say that you had $55 000 in mind but that you would settle for $53 000. Then see what the dealer says.

If the dealer does not offer you anywhere near what you think your collection is worth, say that you are disappointed and ask for a price breakdown item by item. You should be making a considerable profit on your early purchases, while you could be making a loss on your later purchases. If the price you are offered is still disappointing, there could be good reasons, including:

- Most collectors start in a small way and build up their collections as their funds and confidence increase. Hence the bulk of the value usually lies in the most recent purchases, which show the lowest return.

- The dealer has been overcharging you. This would be unfortunate, but you are supposed to know your collection and its worth, and presumably contact with other dealers would have alerted you to this, so it is a case of caveat emptor (let the buyer beware).

- Your feeling for the state of the market is too optimistic.

- You have overestimated the quality or condition of your collection.

- The dealer is trying to get your collection cheaply. In this case go to other dealers.

When it comes time to sell a collectable, you should bear in mind that auction houses are locked into fixed sales calendars, whereas a dealer can commence marketing a collectable from the time it is received. By selling through a dealer you have more control over the final price and the conditions of sale. A dealer can protect you with confidentiality and relative privacy, and avoid the possible overexposure that can arise through auctions.

When selling in conjunction with a dealer you have two choices. You can either make an outright sale or you can sell on consignment. Outright sale is the quickest way to receive cash, but as a dealer has to invest their working capital without a guarantee of a quick return, you will have to settle for less. Selling on consignment entails a dealer working on a commission basis and you are paid when the collectable is sold. Because the dealer has possession of your collectable until it is sold and you are paid, it is vital that you choose someone you can trust. The costs of selling on consignment are generally around 20 per cent or less and comparable with selling at auction, although dealers frequently absorb extra costs, such as photography, catalogue illustration and insurance. If a dealer is competent and they have a little bit of luck, they may be able to achieve a more favourable outcome than when selling at auction. A word of warning, though: do not be in too much of a hurry.

Did you know ... There are advantages and disadvantages of selling at auction compared with selling on consignment. If you sell through a dealer, then the market is limited to the number of people visiting their shop, so be sure to choose a well-known one.

If you choose to sell on consignment, you will have to set a price. Here you will need to be guided by the dealer through whom you sell your collectable. It is a good idea to obtain several opinions and to check the internet and auction results. Ask the dealer to explain their valuation strategy as there are many factors that affect fair market value. Keep in mind that it is in the dealer's best interests (as well as yours) to achieve the highest possible price but the market has practical limits. A collectable can only be sold if there is a willing buyer and a willing seller and a fair price that is acceptable to both.

Fascinating collectables ...

Television annuals

Television annuals were popular between 1960 and 1990 before VCRs and DVD players took off. They attracted children in the eight to 15 age group who could relive their favourite television programs, and many annuals survived into their adulthood. They were usually published in large numbers in the UK and distributed throughout Australia and New Zealand. It is unusual to find annuals with an Australian content, except where a television program was well-known internationally such as *Skippy*, which was produced in the 1970s, and *Neighbours*, whose annuals were produced after 1988.

Second-hand annuals were freely available in flea markets, garage sales, op shops and second-hand bookshops until the 1980s when collectors started buying them. In 2006 the Powerhouse Museum in Sydney featured television annuals in an exhibition commemorating 50 years of Australian television. The most sought after annuals in the 1960s, 1970s and 1980s were those of *Star Trek*, *Dr Who*, *The Goodies*, *Thunderbirds*, *The Avengers*, *Charlie's Angels*, *Starsky and Hutch*, *The Dukes of Hazzard*, *The Jetsons* and *The Beverly Hillbillies*. Copies of these top-shelf annuals sell on eBay today for as much as $100 provided they are in good condition. Bearing in mind that they cost $0.25 to $0.50 second-hand 25 to 40 years earlier, this is a good profit.

Less sought-after annuals sell for lower prices. *The Avengers'* annuals fluctuate in price depending on who the female co-star was. In 1968 the co-star was lesser known Linda Thorson from Canada and that annual is worth about $25. When the co-star was Honor Blackman or Diana Rigg, the annuals were worth more.

Other considerations

Dealers can provide expert valuations of your collectables for such purposes as insurance, legal matters (for example, divorce settlements), CGT, donations and estate planning. The purpose of a valuation will influence how an expert approaches it. Dealers are sensitive to the nuances of different types of valuations and they are competent in interpreting sales information, both public and private. For example, competent dealers can explain why two apparently similar items can sell at different prices.

Be aware that auction results and internet price guides rarely provide enough information to assess the true worth of a collectable. An evaluation of value depends on numerous factors, including quality, condition, rarity, provenance and evolving market conditions. To the untrained eye, vastly different prices may be paid for what appear to be similar collectables. A good dealer will explain to you how prices are determined and why they vary so much. This can have fundamental repercussions on investment potential. In general, a knowledgeable and up-to-date dealer is well placed to assess prices in terms of a collectable's potential for capital appreciation.

Dealers can also assist you with estate planning. A dealer can aid collectors, lawyers and executors to develop a strategy for achieving the highest price if a collection is to be sold, or for dividing a collection fairly among multiple beneficiaries. Often a collector's heirs and personal legal representatives are less knowledgeable about a collection than the person who formed it, and it is therefore wise to involve a trusted dealer when planning your estate. Many dealers also have substantial experience in preparing CGT valuations and dealing with the ATO on related matters.

Did you know ...

Art dealers in Australia tend not to group together like they often do overseas, so you will need to approach them individually.

Art dealers

More so than with many collectables, art is a matter of personal taste. However, the markets treat art as they do any other commodity and the business of investing in art is based on the principle that you buy a painting or print with the expectation that it will increase in value. Otherwise, you should be waiting for its price to fall and to buy it more cheaply. Success in the art marketplace is not easy. There are many artists and many different art forms, and the sheer quantity of artworks, media, periods and styles can make for an intimidating task. Values can rise and fall alarmingly. Nevertheless, if you are prepared to do your homework, investing in art can be lucrative.

In Australia today art is recognised as a strong emerging market in which there is international as well as domestic interest. From 1997 to 2007 art sold at auctions in Australia increased steadily, and in 2007 it fetched $175 million, up from $105 million the previous year, representing an increase of 66.7 per cent. This market fell back to $108 million in 2008 and to $88.2 million in 2009, sparking suggestions that the 2007 figure might be regarded as an aberration. The total art market in 2008, including primary sales through galleries, art consultants and private treaty sales, none of which are formally recorded, was considered by Art Equity Pty Ltd to be closer to $500 million.

Did you know ...

With the introduction of the *Resale Royalty Right for Visual Artists Act 2009* and the role played by CAL in keeping records, more accurate information on the art market will be available in future years.

Like other dealers, art dealers are a goldmine of knowledge, information and advice. However, like other dealers, they are in business to make a profit and therefore they have a preference for selling their own stock. The art business is about profitability as much as it is about art.

Art dealers provide an important function in educating prospective and established clients. They have their own galleries, and many art dealers accompany collectors to artists' studios, museums, art fairs, auctions, exhibitions and other galleries in order to encourage a well-informed approach to art acquisition and sale. Art dealers advise collectors about lending and donating art, insurance, framing, conservation, cataloguing and other subjects of mutual interest.

Exhibitions are central to the way that dealers function. Most artists began with an exhibition at a gallery, and dealers use exhibitions to introduce an artist's new work to the public and to support the development of more established artists. Browsing galleries is one of the most effective ways for you to learn about art and all public galleries welcome visitors during normal business hours.

Many dealers publish exhibition catalogues and monographs as well as newsletters promoting research and critical understanding in areas rarely covered by commercial publications. These are often free and they are a good way of keeping up to date with the art world.

Dealers will assist you in developing a strategy and focus for your collection. They are also instrumental in collaborating with galleries and museums for the purposes of lending artwork to them for exhibitions or safekeeping. It is relevant to note that collectors who understand the custodial relationships inherent in caring for and lending their art to important exhibitions will often be treated more favourably by dealers and artists.

As with collectables the first person you should approach when you wish to sell an artwork is the dealer from whom you bought it (assuming you did indeed buy it from a dealer). Dealers frequently keep track of specific works on behalf of clients and they could even have potential buyers for your artwork in mind when you approach them. Even if they don't, they will appreciate your approach and it will foster a good working relationship. However, do not be afraid to approach several dealers if you are disappointed with the price you are offered.

Providing there is a prospect of doing business, art dealers are passionate about the art and artists they represent and they are enthusiastic about sharing their knowledge with collectors. A good dealer will consider time spent with beginners and established clients equally rewarding and an investment for the future. Engage dealers in conversation about artwork and artists you like and ask questions. You can profit immensely from an ongoing relationship with a good dealer who has your collecting and investment interests in mind.

Art rental dealers

As discussed in chapter 2, providing you have a suitable painting, there is an opportunity to derive rental income from it while you remain the owner. However, you will need to select your artwork carefully and consult with an organisation that offers this facility before you make a purchase. Not all paintings are suitable for rental, so you may find the choice limiting. Only become involved in an art rental arrangement if you genuinely like the painting you are renting out and you are happy to hang it on one of your own walls at the end of the rental period. Although you may be able to renegotiate a rental agreement with someone else at the end of the rental period, or perhaps sell the painting, there are no guarantees and you may be left with an artwork that no longer appeals to you.

The return from art rentals is about 7 per cent to 8 per cent per annum before tax and this is guaranteed by the company that arranges the rental. This is for a period of two to three years and it is exclusive of capital appreciation. The value of suitable paintings starts from about $10 000.

Did you know ... Art rentals can be negatively geared, so a return of 7 per cent to 8 per cent per annum might be considered conservative.

The art rental market is growing as corporations and other organisations seek to turn over the artwork on display in their offices every few years. Since they are attracted by the opportunity to update their artwork, there is no prospect that you could re-let an artwork to the same organisation, but you may find a comparable one that is interested. As explained in chapter 5, you can significantly boost returns from art rentals through negative gearing.

There are dishonest art rental dealers in practice. For example, it has been known that fraudsters have sold the same artwork more than once to unsuspecting buyers. Ultimately it is your responsibility to ensure that you are not being misled. There are obvious dangers if you entrust your collectables with someone else and you also rely on them for professional advice and then they turn out to be dishonest or get into financial difficulties.

Key points

- To buy and sell well privately you need to become your own dealer. This requires you to be knowledgeable and proactive.

- Thoroughly do your homework and research your area of interest, and then specialise in a specific area, region or time period.

- The main advantage of dealing privately is that you eliminate the middlemen and you can save more than 50 per cent of the cost of a collectable.

- Become comfortable in your relationships with dealers, but keep in mind that they will be reluctant to share their knowledge with you and give advice if you do not make purchases from them.

- Inform dealers about what you are interested in so that they can keep an eye out for collectables coming into stock.

- When selling initially, approach the dealer you bought the item from and ask them to make an offer.

- Dealers do more than just buy and sell. For example, they can provide valuations for insurance, CGT and estate planning matters.

- Consider joining associations or clubs as you will probably obtain better deals and you will avoid the dealers' mark-up.

Buying and selling at auction

Auction houses such as Christies, Sotheby's and Bonhams & Goodman have been around for centuries, but auctions on a small scale have only really taken off in the last 30 years. Nowadays it is common to encounter auctions where some items, including collectables, change hands for less than $100. For example, the ABC television program *Collectors* regularly features segments where one of the panelists buys an item such as a toy car in its original box at a local market for $20 and sells it at auction for $50. If commission is 20 per cent ($10), this is a profit of $20 or a return on investment of 100 per cent. If you were to extend this strategy and multiply it many times over, it is clear that there is money to be made.

As well as providing a medium for the exchange of collectables, auctions provide a vital history of values that you can refer to when making decisions about what to buy and sell. Even if you choose not to buy and sell at auction, the information they generate is enormously helpful for making prudent investment decisions; for example, they may provide evidence of fair value at a point in time. From auction results over time you can identify trends that can form a basis for the choice of collectables in which you invest. This chapter looks at auction processes with an emphasis on buying and selling.

Background

Auctions can be exciting, fun and profitable, but at the same time they are a gamble for both buyers and sellers and they can be stressful. For a buyer there is a risk of getting caught up in a bidding war and overpaying for an item. For a seller there is a chance that their lot will not sell and they will be no better off than before the auction. Also, the price that is set for an item may be influenced by emotion and irrational forces, which you would not encounter with a more considered sale through a dealer or in a private situation. Basically, you do not have as much control if you buy and sell through auctions.

For a buyer an auction may be the only opportunity to acquire a much-wanted item and for a seller it may be the best opportunity to obtain a high price. There are advantages and disadvantages and it is best to seek the opinion of experts, such as consultants, dealers, and valuers, before you make up your mind. Auction houses have a vested interest in buyers and sellers going to auction, so treat their advice with scepticism.

Before you make your decision to go to auction you should attend a few to gain a feel for them and to learn more about your collectables and assess their value. Auctions of many types are held regularly throughout Australia and you will find advertisements for them in your local newspaper or via the internet through a search engine such as Google. For example, if you live in Adelaide, type 'Auctions Adelaide' into Google and a list of auction houses in and around Adelaide will come up. As an example, one auction house that will be revealed is Small & Whitfield <www.smallandwhitfield.com> and you can go directly to their website, which will provide details of upcoming auctions including special features.

At any one time there are many auctions taking place around Australia and you can usually find out about them via the internet. Item lists are also often available online, but for major auction houses you will have to buy a catalogue.

Buying at auction

Major auctions are well publicised and you are able to learn about, and view, the items up for sale well in advance. As a buyer you may have an opportunity to buy something you really want that is not available elsewhere. One drawback is that you may 'win' the bidding only to find out that the item did not reach its reserve. You will then have to negotiate privately with the seller. On the other hand, your winning bid could be higher than the reserve and at that price it still represents good value (because the reserve was low). Interest at the time of the auction can play an important role in the bidding process. For example, it has been known for an item to be purchased for an amount at one auction when there were no bidders, only for it to sell for a price higher than the reserve at the next auction.

You may attend an estate auction, which means that most or all of the items for sale come from the estate of one person or family. In other cases an auction house may take consignments from a variety of sources to put together enough items to generate interest from bidders. One type of auction is not necessarily better than the other, but with an estate auction it can be easier to find out the history of an item and you can gain a better idea of provenance. However, note that not everything that is in the estate of an older person is necessarily old or of value.

Auction catalogues

When considering auctions as a means of buying collectables, you should first obtain a copy of the auction house's catalogue. Catalogues range from a basic printed listing of items on an A4 sheet to elaborate glossy publications, which you will have to buy. In the latter case the best way to buy catalogues is to subscribe to an auction house directly. You will usually be able to get a substantial discount from the single-copy price if you sign up for a series. Successful dealers and collectors file and cross-reference catalogues and keep them indefinitely, so you should always keep catalogues, however minor the auctions.

Major auction houses such as Christies, Sotheby's and Bonhams & Goodman print their catalogues well before the auction. You may receive your catalogue three or more weeks prior to an auction and the market could have shifted significantly by the time the sale comes around. This alone could result in a wide discrepancy between price estimates in the catalogue and the prices realised at auction.

To save space, most catalogues use a form of shorthand, which is usually explained in a glossary. Make sure you read and understand this. At major auctions—for example, those held by Sotheby's, Christies, Bonhams & Goodman, Deutscher and Hackett, Deutscher-Menzies, Lawson-Menzies, and Mossgreen—catalogues will contain price range estimates and it is useful to compare these estimates with actual results. If you are a serious collector, you should subscribe to online reference material. For example, the Australian Art Sales Digest <www.aasd.com. au> gives all auction results in Australia by artists for the last 40 years.

Did you know ... There are several sources of information for auction results but they require paid subscriptions.

Something to watch out for at auctions is 'A' lots. These are items that arrive after a catalogue has been published and their details are then printed on an additional sheet that is distributed at the auction. One problem with 'A' lots is that there is no time for expert opinion and therefore the risk that an item is a forgery is increased. If you have bought a forgery, you might not find out until you try to sell it.

Dates

When considering the dates printed within catalogues, note that few paintings are dated by the artist, so the dating is probably done by the auctioneer and it may not be precise. The absence of a date in an otherwise dated catalogue may suggest that a piece is modern. The word 'circa' followed by a date indicates that a work was done at approximately that time.

Measurements

Prints and drawings are measured in millimetres but other objects may or may not be described in metric terms. Paintings are usually measured in centimetres. Measurements are important because size is one of the hardest things to assess when buying collectables if you have not seen the item in real life. For example, you need to appreciate the size of an item to develop a feel for how it will fit with your surroundings.

Condition

The condition of an item is a highly subjective area: one person's tiny chip may be another's total disaster. The absence of a condition report in a catalogue may mean that an item is in perfect condition or it may mean that it is a total write-off. The only viable solution is to question the auctioneer or, better still, make your own inspection.

Attribution

Attribution is a tricky issue because an attribution by one expert may be hotly contested by another. The words 'attributed to' in a catalogue should always sound a warning signal. The problem when an item is 'attributed to' a particular artist or maker is that there is no guarantee that the work or object is by that particular person or maker. The words 'attributed to' introduce doubt about the authenticity of a work or item and you should make doubly sure that you know who is responsible for the item before you buy it.

Type of work

The technique and material used to produce an artwork can affect its price. Types of work include gouache, water colour, monotype, print, drawing and lithograph. The type of work will affect the value. For example, a print would generally be worth less than an oil painting by the same artist. Also, the lower the print number, the higher the value, other things being equal. Works on paper are worth less than works on canvas or board because of the fragile nature of paper.

Provenance

Provenance is the concept of establishing a chain of ownership and authenticity. This is important in preventing fraud and may be of historical interest as well. For major items it is usually possible to find out who the previous owners of an item have been, but in general it is always an advantage to know the chain of ownership. It provides comfort that an item is genuine and sometimes the history of ownership of an item is as important as the item itself. For example, a set of coffee mugs may not have much intrinsic value but if it can be proved that they were owned by Michael Jackson, their value would skyrocket.

Did you know ...

Provenance of an item is more likely to be made known if it is expensive rather than something that is cheap. In the latter case, no-one cares.

Viewing

Attending auctions can be a thrill but getting the most out of the experience requires preparation. Doing well at an auction does not just mean showing up and bidding. An astute buyer takes time to learn about collectables ahead of the auction and how to become an informed bidder rather than an emotional bidder.

Most auctions have previews, which provide a great opportunity for preparation. The preview may be for just an hour or two before the auction begins or it may be held for days before an auction. If the preview time is not listed in the auction advertisement, contact the auctioneer or auction house for details.

If possible attend the preview well ahead of the auction, as close to auction time there will be many other viewers who may get in the way. Also, you may see items that you need time to research further.

While attending the preview there will probably be a few items you have a particular interest in, but take the time to look through everything and at least glance at things that you think you have no interest in. For some items the preview may be the only chance you ever have to look at them in real life. As you go through the items, jot down notes about the ones that interest you, along with their condition and questions you may want to ask. It is important at this stage to note the price you are willing to bid, as it will help you avoid too much emotional bidding at the auction. Bidders have been known to let emotion and competition raise the price well beyond sensible value, which is something you will not want to have to explain to your partner or be accountable for later.

If you are attending a preview of a major auction house and an item interests you, contact the client services department and endeavour to informally discuss how strong the interest is. This is a useful way to get some free advice.

Quality and condition

The preview is the time to judge quality and condition. Some items look much better in real life while others look better in photographs. Size is especially difficult to judge from a photograph. Take a notebook and pen and a magnifying glass with you. A camera is a good idea, especially if the preview is at least a day before the auction. As you gain experience you may wish to also take a penlight, which can be useful for determining the age and composition of glass as well as for spotting repairs.

If you are welcome to physically check the condition of an item, use your hands as well as your eyes. Running your fingers around an object can pick up irregularities that you would otherwise miss. This extra time also helps you determine which items initially appealed to you because they were just odd rather than because they had an enduring interest. You may end up buying items that you will sell in a year or two, or sooner, but you do not want to pay too much for them. If you are welcome to pick up and hold items and check them for condition and damage, handle them with care with both hands. Do not use an item's handle, which if cracked can break, and make sure you put an item back in the place you found it as it may be part of a larger lot.

Did you know ... The preview process is part of the fun about attending auctions. You get to see all manner of things that you would never otherwise see. Often it is interesting to see what they sell for. Enjoy!

Auction houses do not give refunds for faulty goods. You pay for what you see and that makes it doubly important to attend the preview and have a chance to examine collectables up close. If an antique plate has a hairline fracture, it is your job to see it, not the auctioneer's. You may have an opportunity to buy from a catalogue without viewing an item; however, it is essential if at all possible to view any items before you buy them or to consult with an authority that can assess damage and condition.

At the auction

Make sure you know where an auction is being held and check beforehand about which payment methods are allowed. Some auction houses charge an administration fee for the use of a credit card, so be prepared to pay by cash or debit card. Ask if cheques are acceptable and if so, what arrangements you have to make. You will probably have to wait until your cheque is cleared before you can pick up your goods. If you are a regular buyer, you can create an account. Payment is usually made at the end of an auction, but some auctions allow you to pay after you have bought your goods and take possession of them then.

Note whether the auction is a 'reserved' or an 'unreserved' one. If it is an unreserved auction, it simply means that items will be sold to the highest bidder regardless of how low the bid may be; for example $1. At a reserved auction the seller and the auction house agree on a price below which an item will not be sold.

Ask about the provisions you will have to make for picking up items that you might buy at the auction. If it is a small item, then there is no problem, but if it is a piece of furniture, then you will need to make transport arrangements.

Auctioneers and auction houses will be happy to answer your questions, but make sure you ask them ahead of time. Asking questions at the time you bid or make payment is inappropriate as you should know the answers by then.

Bidding at auction

Having thoroughly researched the collectables you are interested in, there are certain strategies you can follow at auctions that will give you the best chance of obtaining a collectable at a good price. For a start, do not get carried away by the moment. Set upper limits on your chosen items and stick to them. If you are not confident you can do this, get someone else to bid for you. Note that nowadays there is a buyer's premium at most auctions, which is 10 per cent to 20 per cent, and this has to be added to the purchase price when you are setting your limits. For example, if the hammer price is $2000 and the buyer's premium is 15 per cent, the price to you is $2300 ($2000 + 15 per cent).

Did you know ...

If you buy an item at auction and also sell it at auction, you will be liable for commissions of upwards of 27.5 per cent. This compares with a dealer's mark-up of 33 per cent to 50 per cent or more.

Arrive at the auction venue early, especially if it will be a long auction and you want a seat. If you intend on bidding, you will generally have to register with the auction house first. They will give you a numbered card which identifies you when you make a bid and which is noted if you are the successful bidder. Then follow early lots and note down the prices in your catalogue. This will give you a useful feel for the performance of the market against the price estimates. When the auctioneer calls the lot number(s) you are interested in, do not jump in immediately; let someone else make the initial running.

When you want to bid, attract the auctioneer's attention by raising your hand, your catalogue, card or paddle, which is provided by the auction house. If the bidding is lively, the auctioneer may ignore you because they can only take bids from two places at a time. Do not worry; if you still want to bid, keep your hand, catalogue, card or paddle in the air and the auctioneer will get around to you. When the auctioneer does take a bid from you, any subsequent nod, wink or twitched finger is enough to indicate you are still in the running. When you have reached your limit, shake your head and the auctioneer will sell to someone else, providing that the item has reached its reserve.

If you are the highest bidder, and your bid is equal to the reserve or higher, the hammer comes down and you are the new owner. There is no cooling-off period. You cannot take the item home, find that it does not fit with your surroundings and take it back. Once your name and the price are recorded, a legally binding contract has been entered into between you and the previous owner. The auctioneer is an agent only and there is no contract with this person, but they are the ones who will pursue you through the courts if you default on your purchase.

It is important that you have an idea of who else is bidding for the lot you are interested in. For example, if a well-known dealer or collector is bidding for the same item, this should give you confidence that the collectable is a good one. Also, the practices of telephone and online bidding have become more popular in recent years. Auctioneers have a love–hate relationship with this process. They hate it because it slows down an auction, thereby reducing momentum, but they love it because it adds mystique and facilitates overseas purchases.

Most auction houses state in their conditions of sale that you are responsible for items purchased immediately on the fall of the hammer. However, some auction houses give you a few days or a week to collect items. If you cannot collect immediately and you have bought a valuable item, it is a good idea to arrange insurance promptly.

Did you know ...

If you are indeed the winning bidder at an auction, make sure you have something to celebrate afterwards and that you have not paid an outrageous price for your collectable.

If you have been outbid on an item and you wish you had bid higher, approach the auctioneer about contacting the winning buyer to see if they are willing to sell to you. This will sometimes work because if it is a dealer, for example, the prospect of making a profit before they have even paid for an item will be attractive. However, if it is a private buyer, they probably want the item as much as you do and they are therefore unlikely to sell.

If you feel the need to question auction room procedures, contact the Auctioneers & Valuers Association of Australia (AVAA): <www. avaa.com.au>, telephone (02) 8765 1573, email aucval@atu.com.au. Membership of the AVAA is voluntary and comprises corporations, sole traders, auctioneers, valuers, and associate and life members. Corporate and sole trader auctioneers and valuers are required to hold professional indemnity insurance. The AVAA is governed by a constitution ratified by the Australian Securities & Investments Commission (ASIC) and all members are bound by a Code of Ethics. Any member who breaches the AVAA's Code of Ethics is liable to disciplinary action.

Selling at auction

Certain auctioneers specialise in particular areas while others are more general in orientation. Depending on the make-up of your holding of collectables, you should have an idea of which auction houses specialise in your area. When selling at auction, contact two or three of them by telephone and ask to speak to the head of the department personally. This is your first contact with an auction house that will potentially be selling your collectables and you should commence evaluating them right from the start. If the person you have called is doing a good job, depending on the value and type of your collectables, they will make an appointment to view them (or if not the head of the department personally, then some other qualified person belonging to the auction house).

If you ask two or three auction houses to report on your collectables, it is a good idea not to let them know that you have approached other auction houses. The reason is that they may be tempted to value your collectables at a higher price in the hope that they will get your business, when obviously what you need is a realistic estimate. You may be given some idea of value on the spot, but more often the auction house representative will take notes and photographs and return to their office to research past prices, and will contact you later with prices. Many auction houses, for example, Christies, will store your collectables at no cost if you commit to auction with them.

The first price estimates you are given may be updated as your collectables are catalogued. If there is a sizeable reduction, it may be because the auction house has made a mistake, or it may be because the expert who visited you has over quoted the value of your collectables to ensure that they get your business. If you are not happy about this, there is little you can do except go to another auction house, where the same thing might happen. In the end, your choice of auction house will depend on the:

- professionalism of the expert who visited you and the rapport you have with them

- quality of previous catalogues

- reputation of the auction house

- conditions of the contract.

The auctioneer's commission is generally payable by the seller and it varies from auction house to auction house and time to time, but 17.5 per cent of the hammer price may be taken as a guide. Hence, if the hammer price of your item is $1000, the auctioneer's commission is $175 (17.5 per cent × $1000) and you receive $825, out of which you have to pay expenses such as photography (if any). As a guide to photography costs, they will be in the vicinity of $250 if your collectable is featured in the catalogue. For example, if you are selling an antique French cabinet for $10000 or more.

As already mentioned there is often a buyer's premium as well, which may be 10 per cent to 20 per cent of the hammer price, so an auction house can make as much as 37.5 per cent on a sale (17.5 per cent selling commission plus 20 per cent buyer's premium); however, if the buyer's premium is 20 per cent, the selling commission may be reduced; for example, to 10 per cent. The idea behind this is to attract more sellers to the auction. The auctioneer is paid the same no matter what Australian state or territory you are in, although major auction houses conduct most of their big auctions in Melbourne and Sydney.

The price estimate range of each lot is either printed in the catalogue or handed out on a separate sheet and is a guide for prospective purchasers. It implies neither an upper nor a lower limit. Clearly, no owner would wish for an upper limit on price, but to protect a lot from going too cheaply a reserve is set. The relationship of the reserve to the price estimates is governed by the auction house, expert opinion (if any), state of the market and the owner. Many auction houses will not charge a commission on unsold lots if the reserves are agreed at their suggested levels.

Did you know ... Auction house practices vary widely, so make sure you know what the policy is with the one you are using. For example, at smaller auctions, the auction house might let you set the reserve without trying to influence your opinion.

When it comes time for an auction, the auctioneer may agree with the owner that the auctioneer be able to exercise discretion with regard to the reserve. For example, an auctioneer may sell at 'reserve with discretion', which means that the auctioneer will aim for the agreed figure but they will sell for up to 10 per cent below it if there is a risk of an item not selling. Also there is the concept of 'selling on the net', which means that an auctioneer can sell below the reserve providing that you do not lose by doing this. For example, if your item is sold for the reserve, you will receive that figure less commission and expenses; however, the auctioneer may cut his own commission and sell for less than the reserve and you will receive the same equivalent figure.

Illustrations in catalogues are arranged by the auction house and range from shared black and white photographs to single-item colour pages to no photographs at all. You are less likely to be able to negotiate photographic charges than commission. With some auction houses, for example, Christies, signing the contract gives them a free hand to illustrate your lots up to a certain figure. Others, such as Sotheby's, agree on the figure at the time of signing the contract.

It is your responsibility to get your collectables to the auction house or its nearest office, unless it provides a free collection service. If not, the auction house can recommend a good local carrier—it is better to use a good one rather than a cheap one. If the expert who initially visits you to view your collection comes by car, you can make up your mind on the spot whether you want to do business with them and, if it is feasible, they may be able to take the property back with them. Insurance is usually agreed on by you and the auction house at reserve price or halfway between the upper and lower price estimates.

Make sure that you clearly understand all terms before signing the contract. The contract is usually in the form of a letter or form, which sets out the commission structure, price estimates, suggested reserves, illustration charges and any other costs or relevant information. You can expect to receive a copy of the catalogue before the auction. Some auction houses will have already confirmed your agreed reserves or, if not yet fixed, they will be when you receive the contract.

Other considerations

If you have become known as a collector, you may be asked by the auction house if it can place your name in the catalogue. This is a personal decision but unless there are good reasons to remain anonymous, it could be good publicity as your name is considered part of the provenance of an item.

If your item fails to sell, you can have it back or it can be entered in the next auction. One alternative is to approach a dealer about selling it on consignment (for details, see chapter 9). If the item is entered into another auction, you will need to review the reserve to see if it was set too high. This is especially important as there is a good chance that your item will be recognised the second time around, so buyers might be less likely to make a bid on it.

Carefully consider whether it is worth spending money on restoration before an auction. The money spent on restoring an item prior to sale may be wasted because buyers generally prefer to make up their own mind about condition and restoration and your work may be for no gain.

Fascinating collectables ...

Surfing memorabilia

The surfing craze that swept through the US and Australia during the early part of the 1960s has given rise to a wide range of memorabilia. Vintage surfboards now sell for thousands of dollars at auction. The items traded are not limited to surfboards—for example, vintage surfboard wax, which cost less than $5 a pack back in the 1960s, can sell for $150 or more if it is unused in its original wrapper. Other items that have significantly increased in value include skateboards (worth up to $300), skimboards (worth about $100), antique surf-o-planes ($200), original surfing magazines (up to $400), surfing movie posters (up to $350) and stickers. Memorabilia from before the 1960s is even more valuable. For example, a hollow construction surfboard from the 1940s could be expected to bring more than $5000 at auction today.

The surfing craze had its own music, which peaked around 1963 when 80 per cent of the Top 10 hits on Australian charts were surfing songs, but they were 'wiped out' by Beatlemania. However, surfing music continued on into the 1970s. American groups such as the Beach Boys, Jan and Dean, and the Surfaris were popular, while in Australia the Atlantics, the Sunsets and the Delltones played surfing songs. EPs and LPs of these artists are worth $50 to $100 today, while an especially rare 1996 EP by the Sunsets (which later became Tamam Shud) called *A Life in the Sun* is worth up to $1000. An EP by the Joy Boys called *Murphy the Surfie* is also rare and sells for around $300. Surfing movie soundtracks are also collectable and valuable. For example, a signed copy of the soundtrack of *Morning of the Earth* is worth $500 to $1000.

Did you know ...

If you are the seller at an auction, the ideal situation is that the item is sold the first time, providing the price is not set too low.

The global financial crisis and collectables

On 3 February 2010 Sotheby's in London held the first major art auction for that year. Although the effects of the global financial crisis have been mild in Australia, there have been profound repercussions in Europe and the US and there were concerns that it would negatively impact on the markets for collectables. In the catalogue for the auction, Lot 8 was described as follows:

PROPERTY FORMERLY IN THE COLLECTION OF DRESDNER BANK AG

ALBERTO GIACOMETTI
1901–1966
L'HOMME QUIMARCHE I ['Walking Man I']
12 000 000–18 000 000 pounds

Description
Executed in 1960 and cast in bronze in a numbered edition of 6 plus 4 artist's proofs. The present work was cast in 1961 and is a life-time cast.
Inscribed *Alberto Giacometti*, numbered 2/6 and with the foundry mark *Susse Fondeur Paris.*
Bronze

PROVENANCE
Galerie Maeght, Paris (acquired from the artist)
Sidney Janis Gallery, New York (acquired from the above in December 1961)
Mr & Mrs Isidore M Cohen, New York (acquired in 1962)
Dr Milton Ratner, New York
Sidney Janis Gallery, New York (acquired in 1980)
Dresdner Bank AG, Frankfurt (acquired from the above in 1980)

This bronze sculpture sold for UK£65 001 250 (US$104.3 million), including buyer's premium, and in so doing it broke the world record for an artwork at auction previously held by a Picasso. Note that it sold at greater than 360 per cent more than the highest price estimate listed in the catalogue and for more than the entire Australian auction market for art in 2009 of $88.2 million.

Total sales at this Sotheby's auction were UK£146.8 million, of which the Giacometti sculpture accounted for over 44 per cent. The global financial crisis had not impacted on investment in artwork, at least at the high end of the market. Such artworks as the Giacometti sculpture are best sold at auction because the publicity surrounding the auction generates interest and ignites the sale process. Note that Sotheby's commission from the sale, including buyer's premium, would have been in the vicinity of UK£12 million. Note also that the price estimate of UK£12 million to UK£18 million may have been deliberately set low to encourage bidders. This is a common ploy by auction houses, especially on big ticket items.

Speculation

Speculators are opportunists who buy inexpensive items in the hope that they will become more valuable over a short space of time. Examples of speculative collectors' items that have handsomely paid off include early Pop Art, Tiffany lamps, which were originally created around 1895 but really took off in the 1950s, and the work of a group of scruffy Paris painters in the 1890s who later became known as the Impressionists. However, these are the success stories. What you do not hear about are the countless collections of items consigned to people's attics that no-one is going to beat a path to their doorstep for. Basically, the speculative approach is a high-risk strategy but it can pay off.

A speculative approach

In terms of being a speculative investment collector, say you were previewing a country auction and you saw a pile of about a dozen 78 rpm singles from the early Australian jazz period of the 1950s that were being sold as one lot and there was no buyers' premium. You thought you could buy them for less than $60 and sell them in the city for three times as much, as that is where you will find the enthusiasts for this market. To compensate for reselling the records 200 kilometres away your target rate of return was 200 per cent. For argument's sake, let's assume that you got the records for $50 and you paid cash. To work out what price you would have to sell them for to make 200 per cent if the auctioneer's commission on the sale is 20 per cent, you can use the following formula:

Let Y = Sale price needed

Then Y (sale price) = 20%Y (auctioneer's commission) + $50 (cost price) + 200% × $50 (profit)

Y = $187.50

Rounded to $188 as no auctioneer would allow a $0.50 bid.

Auction sale price in the city	$188.00
Less commission (20%)	37.60

Consideration	$150.40
	======

Profit = $100.40 ($150.40 – $50)

Investment = $50

Return on investment (ROI) = $100.40/$50 × 100% = 200.8%

The example is for purposes of illustration only but the concept can be applied to any type of collectable of any value. For instance, it is unlikely that you would travel 200 kilometres to earn $100.40. Following are some more comments on this particular scenario:

- The assumption that the speculator can sell the records for $188 may be unrealistic.

- The best avenue for sale may be an individual or dealer. Also the records may be worth more separately rather than by the dozen if several collectors can be located.

- There is an assumption that the records are in good working order, which will not have been proven until the speculator bought them.

- If collectables cost $500 or more, capital gains tax (CGT) is payable on the profit and if held for less than 12 months, there is no discount.

- The ROI of 200.8 per cent is on one transaction. If this happened every month, the ROI would be 2409.6 per cent per annum (200.8 per cent × 12).

- The strategy followed by the speculator in this example is low risk in one sense in that only put $50 was at risk. Assuming the speculator was planning to be in both the country town and the city for other reasons — that is, not just for the auctions and further sale — little is lost if unsuccessful.

- Remember that speculators are opportunists. If you wish to make money this way, you have to keep a constant lookout for potential deals. Some people have the temperament for this while others do not.

Investing in art at auction

Some art, such as the artworks of established artists, is only sold at auction because this is where it generates the most interest and obtains the best prices. Charitable groups also often auction art to raise money whereas it is unlikely they would do this with other types of collectables that have more specialised appeal. Moreover, art is perhaps the most generally held collectable and it is more likely that it will be sold at an auction than other types of collectables.

Did you know ...

If you go to a single owner, estate, country or general auction, it is likely that there will be some art for sale, whereas other collectables may miss out entirely.

You should always endeavour to attend an art auction preview so that you can make your own assessment of quality and condition. If possible, arrange for a dealer to accompany you as they can provide expert advice. A dealer can also bid for you, which may help keep your emotions out of the process. Unlike an auction house, dealers do not have a vested interest in the outcome of a sale and they are therefore able to offer impartial advice.

Catalogues are frequently inaccurate and do not assume that a work is in good condition just because condition problems are not mentioned in the catalogue. As with other types of collectables, it is a case of caveat emptor—let the buyer beware—and it is up to you to notice if an artwork is damaged. It is especially important to arrange for an expert to preview works you are interested in if you cannot attend the preview in person. If questions arise, a dealer or other expert can engage an independent restorer to provide an additional report. If an artwork is damaged, it can be worthwhile to have it restored but you need to know the cost. The test is whether the price you pay plus restoration costs are exceeded by the value of an artwork once restored and you need expert advice to establish this. In some cases it will be uneconomical to restore an artwork, although it might be worthwhile from an aesthetic point of view.

Pre-sale estimates published in auction catalogues are not necessarily predictive of final auction results or of fair value. Estimates are frequently the result of negotiations between the auction house and the seller, and they may represent wishful thinking on both sides. At other times estimates are intentionally set low to attract bidding. Someone such as a dealer may be able to give you a more accurate estimate. Auction houses rely largely on public sales of supposedly comparable works when setting estimates, whereas a dealer or valuer is also familiar with private sales and often they have more insight into the true value of a work. A dealer who specialises in a particular area can evaluate pre-sale estimates and they may be able to suggest a price to pay for a work in light of current market factors.

Do not be misled at the auction as many factors both objective and subjective can affect the outcome of an auction and events in the auction room may not always be what they seem. A work that sells for a lot less than its price estimate is not necessarily a bargain. If an artwork is going for well below its estimate, it may be that the estimate was too high. Possibly the work is in bad condition, which you should have picked up at the preview. Perhaps attribution is doubtful and other bidders have dropped out because of this. On the other hand, the most expensive works are not necessarily the best. Auction room fever can drive up the prices of lesser works. Seasoned auction participants set a limit beforehand and do their best not to exceed it, no matter how frantic the bidding becomes.

Do your homework before an auction and do not be afraid to enlist the services of an expert to advise you. This will cost you a modest fee, but it is worth paying as it may save you from a far more costly mistake.

Key points

- Attend auctions of items in your speciality as a way of getting a feel for them and also of assessing the value of your collectables.

- Seek the advice of experts before you decide to buy or sell at auction as there may be better alternatives.

- Catalogues are a useful reference source. These can vary from listed A4 sheets of items to elaborate publications.

- Make sure you view items you are interested in and note that with auctions caveat emptor applies: let the buyer beware.

- When you are bidding have an upper limit in mind and stick to it. Do not engage in 'emotional' bidding or get caught up in a bidding war.

- If your collectable does not sell, do not despair but consider whether you might be better served by selling the item privately or through a dealer, rather than going to auction again.

- Avoid restoring items you sell at auction because buyers generally prefer to make up their own minds about the item's condition.

- Pre-sale estimates in catalogues are not always a good indication of final price or of fair value.

- Buying items cheaply and then selling them quickly at a higher price is an opportunity to make a good profit, but it can be a risky strategy. It is always wise to buy items that you genuinely love because if they fall in value, you will still have something you can treasure.

- Consider seeking professional advice from dealers and valuers before you take the plunge at auction. You may be better off selling on consignment or buying from a dealer.

8

Buying and selling online

The internet can be an invaluable resource when dealing in collectables. You can use it to do background research on an artist or maker or type of collectable in which you are interested. You can also use it to locate auction houses and dealers and other sources of supply, and to determine whether an item you are interested in is available. You can also get a great deal of information and advice from the internet, which you can profitably use in the pursuit of collecting—although not all of it is reliable. It is an ideal medium for checking prices, with both the aim of establishing value and in the interests of making a purchase or sale. It also offers access to buyers and sellers from all over the world and sometimes in the most unlikely places, so the potential market is huge. Contact is easily established by email. However, there are also many traps for the unwary. For a start, there are many unscrupulous people using the internet, so you need to be cautious.

No one polices the internet for accuracy, so using it must be approached intelligently and with care. Historical information is only as good as the source from which it comes. Internet sellers may post images of collectables they do not actually have access to, or that are incorrectly described, or that are not authentic. Internet prices need to be understood within the larger contexts of collectables markets and they are often meaningless when you have not seen the collectable in person. Many websites provide listings of online sales, auctions or dealers, but these are often financially subsidised services and they are not screened for quality and reliability.

While the internet can be helpful in researching an acquisition, the actual processes of buying and selling collectables take place in the real world and the steps you need to take are fundamentally the same. The difference is that transactions are essentially completed using a computer with minimum personal interaction. So far in the development of the internet as a buying and selling tool there have not been many successful attempts at selling higher priced collectables. You do not hear about collectables selling for millions of dollars on the internet, although participants in the sale of such an item might use the internet for research. Hence, if you are interested in buying and selling more expensive collectables, you will most probably find the internet unsuitable.

Unlike such items as mass-produced books or consumer durables, most collectables are unique and unless you are buying a low cost item it is not appropriate to simply add an item to your online 'shopping cart' and proceed to the 'checkout'. Likewise, if you are selling a collectable, you have to be prepared to provide a fuller description of an item than you otherwise might do and to answer enquiries from interested buyers. Arranging for payment and delivery is not a straightforward matter either, as a buyer will want to ensure that they receive the items they pay for and a seller will want to ensure that payment is forthcoming before they send an item to the buyer.

Did you know ... Online marketplaces really took off around 2000–01 at the time of the dotcom bubble. While many online start-up companies did not survive this period, those such as eBay thrived and have become valuable resources in the collectables marketplace.

To give you an idea of how vast the area of collectables is on the internet, if you insert the word 'collectables' into Google you will get over 22 million results, including such things as a Wikipedia listing plus myriad sites dealing with collectables. If instead you insert 'collectables online', you will get more than 36 million results relating to every kind of collectable you can possibly think of—the task of deciding where to start is formidable. In this chapter eBay has been chosen for special consideration because it is the biggest and most well-known international marketplace. Note that the principles that apply to good buying and good selling on eBay apply to any online marketplace.

About eBay

eBay was founded as AuctionWeb in San Jose, California, in 1995 by 28-year-old Pierre Omidyar, a French-born Iranian computer programmer. One of the first items sold on eBay was a broken laser pointer for US$14.83. When Omidyar contacted the winning bidder to make sure he knew the laser pointer was broken, the buyer said he was a collector of broken laser pointers! Today eBay exists in more than 30 countries, although it has not been successful in Taiwan or Japan where Yahoo is dominant, or in New Zealand where TradeMe is the main online marketplace. eBay Australia's website is <www.ebay.com.au>.

There are hundreds of millions of registered users on eBay and at the time of writing revenues were US$8.727 billion, with a net income of US$2.389 billion. The number of employees exceeds 15 000 and it is one of the companies that make up the S&P 500 Index. eBay also owns PayPal, which is the preferred payment method on eBay and which offers security to both buyers and sellers. There are a number of prohibited items that cannot be sold on eBay, such as body parts, or anything related to crime; for example, tickets to executions.

The mechanics of buying and selling

From a buying and selling point of view there are three categories on eBay, namely:

- *Auction-style listings.* Where the seller specifies an opening price, which may be as low as $0.01. The seller has the option of specifying a reserve, which is a price below which they will not sell. For example, you might be interested in selling a collectable for which you will not accept less than $200. You could put in any price as the starting bid but if the highest bid is less than $200, you are not obliged to complete the sale. An auction period is set, which in Australia may range from a few days up to 14 days. Buyers bid in increments such as $0.50 and at the end of the auction period the item for sale goes to the highest bidder, providing the reserve has been met. If you set a starting price of $0.99, the chances are that your item will be sold. If you set a higher price, it's possible that it will not sell.

- *Fixed price format.* Where the seller specifies the price they want for an item and the first buyer to offer this price gets the item. Sometimes there are multiple items available at the same price, although this is less usual with collectables, which have a greater tendency to be unique. On eBay this fixed price is referred to as the Buy It Now (BIN) price. Sellers using the auction-style listing have the option of combining it with a BIN price. They can initiate an auction with an opening bid and a specified term and also state a BIN price, which means a buyer can circumvent the auction process by paying the BIN price at any time and obtaining the item regardless of what future bidders are prepared to pay.

- *Fixed price format with best offer.* Where the seller sets a price and invites buyers to make their best offer. If a buyer submits their best offer, the seller can accept or reject it. If they reject it, the buyer can then re-submit their best offer. Best offer is not available for auction-style listings and the best offer format is not available in all categories. Sellers must meet specific requirements to qualify for the best offer format — for example, they cannot be registered as a business or as a Store Subscriber.

Did you know ...

Combining an auction-style listing with a Buy it Now price is popular on eBay as it signals to bidders what the highest possible price is for the item.

When you list an item on eBay you are charged an Insertion Fee for listing the item. If the item sells, you are also charged a Final Value Fee. There are also fees for optional items that help to sell your item; for example, additional photographs. The total cost of selling an item is the Listing Fee plus the Final Value Fee plus any optional features fees. Fees vary depending upon the site and category you are listing your item on.

Selling on eBay

Say you had a glass vase that you had inherited as part of an estate. You were not sure of its value but you had seen a similar one with a dealer for $600. You thought that you would auction it on eBay. Since you would not sell it for less than $500, you set this figure as the reserve, but you hoped that it might fetch more. You take a photograph of the vase and you initiate an auction with a starting bid of, say, $50 and a 14-day term, which is the maximum for an auction-style listing. At the end of 14 days the vase did well and the highest bid was $800. Your fees for selling on eBay would be as follows:

Insertion fee	$3.50
Final value fee	
On the first $75, 5.25%	$3.9375
On the amount between $800 and $75, 2.75%	$19.9375

Total	$27.375
Rounded	$27.38
	======

eBay commission as a percentage of the selling price

$= \$27.38/\$800 \times 100\% = 3.42\%$.

This outcome compares favourably with the commission payable at 'live' auctions of, say, 17.5 per cent, plus such fees as cataloguing expenses. Of course, you still have to arrange delivery with the buyer and since the vase is valuable you could not readily send it through the post. Specifying 'Pick-up only' would be the safest option but this would limit your market, depending on where you live.

ebay's Insertion Fee is based on the value of the starting bid or reserve price, when there is one. From $0.01 to $0.99 the cost is 30 cents, while for amounts above $5000 it is $10. The Final Value Fee is based on the value at which an item changes hands. Up to $75 the cost is 5.25 per cent of the sale price; on the next $925 up to $1000 it is 2.75 per cent and on the excess above that it is 1.50 per cent. For a full breakdown of fees on eBay go to <http://pages.ebay.com.au/help/sell/fees.html>.

eBay guides

There are two types of guides on eBay. The first type are eBay Guides, which are either written by eBay or eBay partners. These always appear with an eBay logo. The second type are Member Guides, which are written by eBay members. To access Guides go to <http://pages.ebay.com.au/learn_more.html> and insert 'collectables' in the search box. A listing of Guides will be displayed with eBay Australia's Guides first. Following are just some of the Buying Guides that will be revealed:

- Sports Cards
- Sports Memorabilia
- Lamps and Lighting
- Pottery and Glass
- Hot Wheels
- Stamps
- Movie and TV Memorabilia
- Music Memorabilia
- Prints
- Militaria
- Magic the Gathering Trading Cards
- Star Wars Action Figures
- Camera Lenses
- Sports Autographs
- Talking Boonie Dolls.

You will also find eBay buying tips at <http://help.ebay.com.au/Help/ Buying/Buying_basics/Smart_buying_tips>.

Member Guides cover a wide range of topics with varying degrees of relevance in making the most out of eBay. Some focus on general topics, while others are concerned with specific traps and tips. The following information is a summary of advice drawn from the experiences of eBay users.

Did you know … Many Member Guides are written by collectors and contain tips and traps for buying and selling based on their own experiences.

Timing auctions for maximum profit

If you are selling by auction on eBay, the two questions you need to address are, firstly, how long should your auction run and, secondly, when should it start/end? A 14-day auction is good as it gives the maximum number of people a chance to participate as opposed to a three-day auction, for example. However, 14 days is a long time for someone who wants the auction to end so that they can take possession of an item and buyers may lose interest. A seven-day auction is better for maintaining interest and it covers every day of the week, including the peak periods of Friday night and Saturday. It is often the case that there is a flurry of bidding activity at the end of an auction, so do not time it to end between 10 pm and 7 am when most people are asleep. Also, the successful bidder may not wish to have to wait a long time for delivery, so do not time the auction to end on Friday night when the earliest that delivery can be made is probably Tuesday of the following week. On the other hand, if it is a pick-up only, Friday may be a good time because the item can be collected on the weekend

A good time to end an auction is between 8 pm and 9 pm Sunday to Thursday because most people are at home and probably not asleep. Sunday night at 9 pm is an especially good end date because goods can be made ready for delivery the next day. Hence, choose a seven-day auction that commences at 9 pm on Sunday night to close the following Sunday at 9 pm.

Starting price and reserve

A low starting price will attract more bids, especially in the first few days. If you start at $0.99, you can expect bids within hours. This does not ensure you will get the price you would like but it is a good start. Potential bidders will be attracted by an auction that already has other bidders. This is analogous to a stall at a local market where if there are hundreds of people milling around it encourages others to have a look and find out what is going on. Setting a low starting price does not prevent you from having a realistic reserve. However, many bidders are turned off by items with reserves because they know that even if they win the auction, they might not get the item. This encourages them to look for auctions where there is no reserve. However, auctions for collectables are a slightly different category because many of the items for sale are unique and there are no alternative auctions available.

Photographs

Take photos of your collectables so that they are clearly visible, along with their condition and any unusual aspects. eBay allows you to include one photo free of charge and if you use your own image hosting service, you can easily include as many photos as necessary to show your collectable in detail. Consider using the gallery option so that the image will appear within the search listings. As a rule you should never attempt to sell an item without at least one photo.

 **Did you know ...**

It is an old cliché but a 'picture is worth a thousand words' and this is true on eBay. Most sellers post photographs and most buyers expect one.

About Me page

Your 'About Me' page provides you with an opportunity to sell yourself by establishing your credibility. A reason someone will not buy from you online is because you have failed to establish credibility, so include your details such as where you are located, the length of time you have been registered on eBay and the areas in which you specialise. Have a look at other About Me pages to see what works.

Returns policy

For collectables it is important that you or a buyer can establish authenticity. One way of doing this is to say you will accept returns if an item can be shown not to be genuine. But make your return policy valid for a specified time; for example, 30 days. At the very least you should have a return policy that covers cases where someone has bought an item that is not as described. Hence, make your descriptions accurate.

Feedback

Leave feedback for the winning bidder as soon as they have completed their side of the transaction. Do not be afraid of getting a neutral or negative comment on your feedback record as most buyers will consider all of your feedback before bidding, not just one or two comments. If you receive negative feedback over something that was your fault—for example, late shipping—admit that it was your fault in response to feedback.

Attending to enquiries

Give fast and accurate replies to bidder enquiries and do not wait several days before responding to emails or telephone calls. Some sellers take too long to respond to straightforward emails. Keep bidders informed about such things as shipping dates or pick-up arrangements.

Delivery

Make sure that the buyer knows what the delivery charges are when they bid for an item. Do not be tempted to overcharge for delivery as it is easily discovered and it is one of the worst things a seller can do, and it is also against eBay policy. If you are using Australia Post, go to <http://auspost.com.au> to calculate charges. Offer the option of insurance, which you can arrange with Australia Post for a fee on some delivery options. Ship items in packages the way you would like to receive them. For example, if you are sending breakable items, make sure they are carefully packed in bubble wrap. A thoughtfully wrapped item will be well received and it will translate into glowing positive feedback from the buyer.

If you are the buyer, note the type of delivery options available when checking out. While most sellers will inform a buyer when an item is shipped, if you have not heard anything, contact the seller for a status update. Standard delivery will usually take three days to reach you, while express delivery will usually reach you on the next business day. Contact the seller if you wish to insure an item and the seller has not indicated this service.

Delivery of collectables can be tricky because they are often fragile. If something is capable of being damaged, ensure that the seller takes all necessary precautions. Otherwise check before you bid if they will allow you to arrange a pick-up.

Buy It Now price

When you list an item for auction you can specify a Buy It Now (BIN) price, which is the amount that you would accept if someone offered it to you after you listed the item. So you might list an item for auction with a starting price of $5 and a BIN price of $20. Instead of participating in the auction process a buyer could offer you $20 upfront and win the item immediately. Your advantage is that you get a price that is acceptable to you without having to wait until the end of the auction period when the price may well not have reached $20. The disadvantage is that you are limiting yourself to a price of $20 when the item may well have sold for more if the auction process had been allowed to play out.

Fascinating collectables ...

Drive-in theatre speakers

The first drive-in theatre in Australia opened in Melbourne in early 1954 and by mid 1956 there were seven drive-ins. Adelaide soon followed Melbourne, but it was a long while before Sydney had a drive-in theatre. Today drive-in memorabilia are popular collectors' items, especially the speakers that were hooked to a car's window. The period from 1954 to the 1980s, when most drive-ins closed (although Melbourne still has three), is considered a unique part of Australia's cinema history and the Performing Arts Museum in Melbourne has a collection of drive-in memorabilia.

When the drive-ins began to close the owners disposed of such things as speakers, selling them for $1 to $2 each in bulk. Nowadays these speakers are worth between $40 and $300 each, depending upon rarity and condition. There are a few serious collectors around, including one or two who have set up their own mini drive-ins. Speakers are worth more in pairs, especially if they are connected to the junction boxes. A single Thompson model speaker is worth about $50, while a Brady speaker is worth about $100 and the RD2 is worth around $300. A Wallis speaker is also worth around $300. These prices reflect rarity and assume good condition. In fact, some collectors prefer speakers to look used because it reflects the history of the drive-in when such objects were exposed to all types of weather and even abuse by patrons.

How to win an eBay auction

It is quite common for bidding towards the end of an online auction, whether it be on eBay or anywhere else, to become frenetic as buyers put in last-minute bids to win an item. You may follow an item for days and bid on it only to find that at the end of the auction your best bid has been beaten. To increase your chances of winning, on eBay you can insert the maximum price you are prepared to bid and eBay will automatically increase your bid by a predetermined amount if your existing bid is overtaken, up to your maximum price (this is referred to as 'proxy bidding', with eBay being the proxy). This process forces you to set an upper limit on an item you are interested in and minimises your chances of bidding beyond your budget. On the other hand, it can be disheartening to fail to win an item you particularly want by as little as $0.50. However, if you have decided you especially want an item, getting involved in a prolonged bidding war with a rival is not what you want either, even if you win. In the process you will have artificially inflated the price and you will have to pay for being the psychological 'winner'.

Auction snipers

The way around many potential bidding problems is to use an 'auction sniper' computer program. You do not have to install the software as there are numerous companies that specialise in this area. To use an auction sniper you first sign up for a service, which may be free if you only make a few bids a week. Then you cut and paste the item(s) you are interested in from eBay onto the auction sniper website and you set your maximum bid price. Note that this still forces you to set an upper limit to your bidding, which you should do in a cool, calm and collected manner. The big difference with using an auction sniper service is that the program only bids for you a few seconds before the auction closes and then only at a price high enough to win the auction, up to your predetermined limit. You effectively avoid a costly bidding war and guarantee yourself the maximum chance of winning, as there is not enough time for someone else to put in a counter bid.

Numerous companies provide an auction sniper service and if you type 'auction sniper' into Google, they will be revealed. One such system is JustSnipe <www.justsnipe.com/auctions/product.asp>, which is a US-based system that supports eBay Australia (as well as most other countries) and bids in Australian dollars at eBay Australia auctions. There are basically two types of plans, including a Free Membership Plan, which entitles you to use the system five times a week for free, and a Value Membership Plan, which entitles you to unlimited use plus other advantages for US$5 per month. If you wish to try it out, the free plan is adequate, although under this plan the bid is made eight seconds before closing whereas under the value plan it is made five seconds before closing. To use JustSnipe you will have to provide your eBay username and eBay password, and you will need to create a username and password for JustSnipe.

Did you know … By using an auction sniper you will avoid a bidding war with others who potentially could be hell-bent on winning the auction rather than owning the item being bid for.

JustSnipe uses a highly advanced computerised bidding system, which is a simple program to use. You log on to JustSnipe and then scan eBay for the items you want and cut and paste the eBay auction numbers that you want to win into JustSnipe. Then all you need to do is enter your maximum bid and the lead time before the auction finishes (minimum eight seconds with the free plan). You do not need to leave your computer switched on for your bid to be executed. There is no guarantee, however, that you will win the auction. For a start, your maximum bid price may not be high enough. Also auction sniper service companies have been around for years and you may be up against another bidder who is using one that has a shorter lead time. For example, if a bidder is using JustSnipe's value plan, their bid will be lodged five seconds before the auction closes, but a random bidder may be lucky and get their bid in one to two seconds before the auction closes. However, regardless of scenarios like this, JustSnipe gives you an excellent chance at success while avoiding a bidding war.

One final thought on bidding using an auction sniper service: if your limit on an item is $200, make it $200.50 when you enter your maximum bid. The reason is that most bidders think of limits in round figures and there is always a chance that $200 may be someone else's limit, too. If at the end of an auction there are two bids of equal value—for example, $200—the person who bid first wins the auction. And if your bid is lodged eight seconds before the end of an auction, in the event of a tie it is unlikely that your bid of $200 will have been made first. However, if you made a maximum bid of $200.50, you would win the auction. This is assuming of course that you need to bid your limit to win the auction in the first place.

Things to watch out for

Shill bidding is a practice used in conjunction with online auctions whereby a seller artificially increases the price or desirability of an item. For example, a seller may arrange for friends, family or work colleagues to bid for an item that makes it appear that there is a lot of interest in an item and also increases its price. In some cases on eBay unscrupulous sellers have been known to have several accounts and they sell an item through one account and bid for it from another account. A legitimate and unsuspecting bidder sees the price steadily rise each time they make a bid. When the price has reached a point that is acceptable to the seller, they stop bidding from their other account. As you would expect, shill bidding is prohibited by eBay but with so many users and transactions it is not always detected and buyers are defrauded. When friends, family and work colleagues are accomplices, shill bidding is even harder to detect and it has been described by experienced eBay users as a 'huge problem'.

The first thing you need to do if you suspect shill bidding on an item is to check the 'Bidders List' for the item you are bidding on. A shill bidding account will usually have very little or no feedback. The account might even have been created in the last 30 days with the sole intention of shill bidding for the seller. If a member is new, they have a small orange icon next to their User ID. Next you should do some research on the seller's other sales via their feedback profile and see if the suspected shill bidder was bidding on those items as well. If so, the chances are that the seller is using a second account or the account of someone they know to shill bid.

Writers of eBay Member Guides state that shill bidding is the biggest problem on eBay.

Another technique to spot shill bidding is to check the increments used to increase the bids. Usually a shill bidder will increase bids by small amounts, which puts the impetus back on you to bid again. The shill bidder will keep on bidding until you stop and they will then retract their bid, leaving you the winning bidder at a price higher than you otherwise would have paid. If you suspect shill bidding, inform eBay and if it finds that shill bidding has occurred, it will suspend all associated accounts.

Scams

There are numerous other scams to watch out for on eBay. They include:

- *False photographs.* It is easy for unscrupulous sellers to post photographs that depict an item that is not the one listed for sale. Know what you are bidding on. Genuine sellers will not be afraid to answer questions or to reveal the correct item.

- *Fakes.* Many fake items are sold via the internet and collectables are especially vulnerable. Ask for a certificate of authenticity or insist that the seller offer a return policy if your own investigation reveals that an item is not the real thing.

- *False feedback.* Be aware that there are computer programs available that can generate a heap of positive feedback for a buyer or seller within a short space of time. That said, beware of sellers with a low feedback rating and plenty of negative comments.

- *Fraudulent use of credit card and bank account details.* This is a major problem when buying goods online. Also, never pay with cash or use wire transfer systems. Use PayPal because at least you have some protection.

- *Buyers not paying.* When you are selling an item, beware of non-payers. You can block bidders that have no feedback or don't have a PayPal account. People who are new to eBay are often the ones who do not pay because they do not understand the process, so be prepared to explain it to them. Only send an item after payment has been received and only refund money after the item has been returned to you.

- *Delivery problems.* A buyer may claim that they never received delivery of an item, so always get proof of postage.

- *Return issues.* Watch out for buyers who purchase an item and then return a substitute, which may be old or broken, and claim a refund.

- *False descriptions.* As a buyer, beware of receiving an item that is not as described. Some people are downright dishonest with their descriptions. Look at feedback descriptions and see if there are any comments to the effect that items were received with faults. It has been known to happen that a buyer has purchased an empty box and had no redress because of a cleverly worded description.

- *Sellers not sending goods.* Be alert to sellers who take payment and never make delivery. Check the seller's feedback and ask the seller to tell you when an item was sent. By using PayPal you will have some security.

- *Deceiving PayPal.* Dishonest buyers can purchase items via PayPal, claim that an item was never received and receive a PayPal refund. Sellers should scrutinise the buyer's feedback carefully to see if there is any evidence of this type of activity, especially before shipping high-value items.

Most of the millions of transactions on eBay are trouble-free, but you need to be on the alert for unscrupulous buyers and sellers.

Art on the internet

So far the risks associated with buying and selling unique higher priced art on unvetted websites such as eBay have been considered too great, so online auctions have not been successful. PayPal cannot wholly protect against disappointment or fraud, and eBay auctions typically take place over a period of days with bids in small increments. In recent times some of the larger auction houses have introduced internet bidding at live auctions. This is essentially the same as bidding by telephone, except that participants use a computer to place bids. Nevertheless most bidding at art auctions is done live in the saleroom.

While online art auctions may not be very common, there are many online galleries and dealers selling art to the public. If you type 'art online australia' into Google, you will get over 54 million results. As an example, one of the websites that will be revealed is AustralianArt Classifieds (AAC), <http://australianart.com.au>, which publishes classified advertisements with the aim of bringing buyers and sellers of art together. AAC does not charge commission on sales but rather charges a modest classified advertising fee. For example, the cost of an art classified advertisement is $30, with an extra $20 if it is a featured advertisement. Bolding costs $5 and for better placement you'll pay $7, with an 'attention getter' advertisement costing an extra $15. Each listing carries with it the right to display four photographs.

Key points

- The internet is a useful resource for researching collectables and for comparing prices, and for providing access to buyers and sellers all over Australia.

- There are many unscrupulous internet users and many scams to watch out for.

- eBay is the biggest and most well-known online marketplace in Australia. It began in 1995 with one person and today it is a global multi-billion-dollar business.

- The fees for selling on eBay are low and there are no buying fees. The commission payable for an online auction is a fraction of the commission that an auction house charges on the same selling price.

- ebay has many Guides that provide useful information.

- It is important to carefully choose the parameters of an auction, including such things as a starting price, reserve (if any), photographs, return policy, delivery and auction period.

- The best way to get around auction problems such as a bidding war is to use an auction sniper service that enables you to bid a matter of seconds prior to the close of an auction.

- Shill bidding, whereby a seller artificially increases the bid amount or desirability of an item, is the biggest single scam on eBay.

- Other scams include false photographs, fakes, false feedback, dishonesty in describing items, and fraudulent use of credit card and bank account details.

- Online auctions of art are not very common, although some auction houses have introduced online bidding, which works like telephone bidding.

Dos and don'ts when buying and selling collectables

In the previous chapters we have examined different aspects of investing in collectables, with information and recommendations on what you should and should not do in pursuing your interest. For example, if you want to make money out of collecting, then quality takes precedence over quantity and you should buy the best you can afford. You may have to wait to accumulate the necessary financial resources, but you are better off doing this because a high-value item will usually appreciate by more, and be easier to sell in both good and bad markets. For example, you might be lucky and buy a painting by an emerging artist who takes off overnight, but this is a very risky strategy and the chances are that it will not happen. This chapter looks at a number of 'do's and don'ts' when buying and selling collectables when an investment return is a major criteria.

Research

The first thing you need to do before you buy and sell collectables is conduct extensive research. Watch television programs, such as *Antiques Roadshow* and *Collectors,* and find out if there are any local radio programs on collectables and memorabilia. For example, Radio 2UE in Sydney has a weekly program *Antiques and Collectables,* which airs at 4 am on Saturday mornings. Read books and magazines and columns in newspapers dealing with collectables. Each Wednesday the *Sydney Morning Herald* publishes a 'Money' lift-out section, which usually contains a column on collectables. When you are researching particular collectables, visit dealers, museums, garage sales, auctions, junk shops, local markets and galleries, essentially wherever they can be found. Talk to knowledgeable people about your area of collecting and what is likely to appreciate in value. Use the internet to research items and their availability and to check prices. 'Live' with your area of collecting through research and develop a feel for what is worth investing in.

Next you should learn about the distinctive qualities of what you collect. Aim to know what makes an item collectable and why it is more valuable than a reproduction. As part of the learning process consider the following highlighted factors.

Rarity

Assess the rarity of a collectable because it is a key determinant of value. Focus on collectables that have a finite supply (of which there are an enormous number of possibilities so this is not an onerous constraint). A painting by a well-known deceased artist will generally appreciate in value with the passage of time because the artist is not around to paint any more. Similarly, high quality rare examples of Egyptian jewellery, Roman coins, prehistoric fossils, Greek vases, shipwreck coins and tribal carvings will nearly always appreciate in value because of their limited supply. Autographs of famous people who are dead will increase in value because they cannot sign any more, as opposed to a living person who can influence supply by signing more autographs.

However, in assessing rarity you have to look further than the age of an item. While the supply of many items will decline with the passage of time because they are lost or get broken or damaged, many old items are not rare. For example, there is a large supply of stamps of some eras that are well over 50 years old. The key in this situation is to look at how they were made.

Did you know ... If you are investing in coins today bought straight from a place such as The Perth Mint, look at how many were minted before outlaying your money. If it is more than a few thousand coins, then it is unlikely to be a good investment for you.

Demand

Demand is another key determinant of value and your aim should be to identify collectables where demand is expanding. But unlike rarity, which can be objectively established, future demand is much more subjective and it can be influenced by what is in fashion. Demand for an item can take off because of unusual external factors related to a specific market. For example, memorabilia associated with Princess Diana became much more in demand after her death. Such events are impossible to predict.

It is sometimes the case that demand for a type of collectable will languish because there are few examples brought to sale. This can happen with makers and artists who may have been active 30 years ago but whose work is not traded. Then a few pieces might be offered for sale at auction, which generates interest and a more lively market is created. Other owners see an opportunity to make a profit and more pieces come onto the market. Demand increases because of the interest generated. Opportunities like this do not come along very often but they do happen and they are something to watch out for. In this case an increase in supply has led to an increase in demand, when it is usually the other way around.

The number of buyers for items of museum quality is increasing, which you should keep in mind for two reasons. Firstly, the trend provides opportunities for profit-making because such items are in finite supply.

Secondly, museums themselves are acquiring these items, which means that the supply available to private collectors is diminishing. An increasing demand combined with a reducing supply means that prices go up. You should watch trends as they develop and build an investment strategy around them.

Condition

Condition is as important as rarity and demand in determining value, so you should check items carefully. Cracks, scratches, chips and other damage and repairs will affect an item's value. In some cases an otherwise valuable item can be made worthless. Bear in mind that if an item's condition is poor, it provides a useful bargaining tool when buying it but at the same time its potential for capital appreciation will be affected. If you are the seller of such an item, the person buying it from you will make the same arguments.

It is preferable to buy a damaged item unrestored with the aim of having it professionally restored, rather than buy an already restored item of dubious standard. This will depend on the item and its intrinsic value and the costs of restoration. Keep in mind that if you intend to on-sell it, the buyer will probably wish to do their own restoration. There is a market for damaged collectables but the important thing to appreciate is the extent of the damage and the impact this will have on value. Clearly, you need an idea of the costs of restoration.

Do not buy an item that has been 'overly restored'. You should aim to buy items that are in as pristine condition as possible. For example, a vase that is 2500 years old may have been repaired or have missing parts, but if this is on the bottom of the vase and does not affect the painted areas, it may be minor; however, if it is the head that is missing, it will really affect its value.

Did you know ... The storage of collectables is important in preventing damage; for example, coins should not touch each other and stamps should be in albums. The storage of wine is especially critical.

Budget

If you are new to collecting, start in a small way but focus on buying the best item you can afford. Set limits on how much you are willing to spend. Buy at auction if you wish to, but be aware that this environment may give you a false sense of security because it is easy to keep bidding in the belief that what you are paying must be fair market value: why else would anyone else be bidding? Be cautious and stick to one or two collecting areas and study the prices paid at auction for the previous 10 years to get an idea of how much items are worth. Compare auction prices with those of dealers.

You can eliminate many areas of collecting because of the amount of money you have to spend. Do not save up for years to buy a collectable with the prospect of staying out of the market for a few years because you do not have enough money to continue collecting. You will not qualify as a collector and it is certainly not the way to make money. Aim to make regular additions to your collection and cash in on opportunities when they arise.

Storage

Use common sense: if you live in an ultramodern apartment, do not collect antique furniture. Likewise it would be impractical to have a wine cellar. If you have young children or a dog, make sure collectables are out of harm's way. Do not hang paintings in direct sunlight. Make sure that rare books are well housed. If you have a rare coin or jewellery collection, you need to store them within a safe at your home or within a safe deposit box at a bank.

Reputable sources

Unless you are buying on the cheap from a place such as a garage sale, you need to know what you are buying, so deal only with reputable sources. Always ask about the provenance of an item because you need to buy items that have a collection history. A reputable dealer, gallery or auction house will have researched authenticity and it will only resell legally exported items. There are many extremely good fake collectables around and some of them are only detectable by experts, so beware.

Garage sales

Attending garage sales is a popular weekend pastime for many collectors. You are likely to pick up bargains at a garage sale, but by the same token they do not qualify as a 'reputable source'. They are a less attractive proposition for selling collectables because prices tend to be kept low. Garage sales range from small events where someone may just be clearing junk out of their home to large-scale ones run by schools or charitable organisations.

Following is a list of dos and don'ts when buying collectables at garage sales:

- Do keep an eye on newspapers, especially local ones, to see when garage sales are held. Sometimes they are advertised on street poles.

- Despite what an advertisement might say, do be prepared to see anything at a garage sale. There are usually many one-off items that the organisers do not think warrant a separate mention and they could be what you are looking for.

- Do have an idea of what you are looking for before you go, but keep an open mind about the unexpected.

- Do get there early. If the advertised starting time is 9 am, get there at 7 am. You will be unwelcome at that time and the sellers may not be ready for you but you will get first look at the goods. Dealers always go early.

- Do have a very good look at what you are buying because you will not be able to return it. If an item has defects, you are the one who has to spot them. Do not be afraid to ask questions of the seller. If something seems too good to be true, it probably is.

- Do make sure you have a good look for collectables that may have been placed out of the way.

- If you are buying with a view to selling (for example, at auction), do make sure an item is saleable with the prospect of a good profit. This is where your research will pay off. If selling on eBay, make sure it is not a prohibited item.

- Do check the items for sale methodically so that you do not miss anything.

- Do not take your children or your dog if you can avoid it.

- Do bring plenty of small change.

- Do bargain but do not do so unreasonably. Ask for a discount if you are buying a number of items.

- Do be polite and smile while you are there, as it will be appreciated. This is especially so if you have arrived at 7 am.

- Do take your business cards because you never know when they might be useful.

- Do bring one or two carrier bags.

- Do consider carefully before parting with a large amount of money as it is easy to get carried away on the spur of the moment. If in doubt, leave your card with the seller and negotiate after the garage sale if the item is not sold.

- If something is too expensive at first, do return later in the day to see if it is still there and try negotiating again. This is especially so if the weather has turned bad.

- Do not take more money with you than you can afford to spend.

- Do have a final look around before you leave.

Much the same list of dos and don'ts applies when buying from junk shops or at local markets or street fairs.

Negotiating

Negotiating over price is an art and it should not degenerate into unreasonable haggling. If that happens, it will cause resentment and unpleasantness on both sides whereas if handled with good intentions — both sides want a sale — and consideration, it can be an enjoyable part of a transaction. In some countries, such as Asia, bargaining is expected for everything from flea market purchases to taxi rides. In other countries, such as Australia, it is not as widespread. Some people have a natural flair for negotiation and enjoy it. If you do not, get someone else to negotiate for you. Note that in some areas you may be able to negotiate prices on services that are ancillary to the item being sold. For example, if you are selling expensive items at auction, you may be able to negotiate illustration costs in the catalogue.

Following are some dos and don'ts if you are a buyer:

- Do be polite and courteous when you offer less than the seller is asking.

- Do not make an outrageously low offer at a garage sale or local market in the expectation that a subsequent higher offer will then be favourably received. Your first offer will cause offence and that is not a good way to start. For example, if a seller is offering a cup and saucer for $50 and you think it is worth about $35, do not offer $10 as this will cause resentment. Offer $25, which still gives you room to move on your best offer. Make your offers ballpark figures.

- Do not expect to be able to bargain with reputable dealers. As discussed in chapter 6 their prices are considered prices and they are not pulled out of the air. You may get a discount for paying cash or for some other reason (for example, a quick sale) but do not assume that they are operating flea markets.

- If an item you want is passed in at auction, do approach the auction house about negotiating with the seller. The seller will be seeking the reserve price, which may not be much higher than the highest bid and you can negotiate from there. The first step is to find out how much the seller wants and the next step is to make an offer closer to this price. When the reality sets in that the item has not sold, the seller may be prepared to come down. Note that you will still have to pay the buyer's premium.

- Do not assume that a seller is stupid but they may be influenced by psychological factors, so endeavour to understand their behaviour and price. Then look for ways around an apparent impasse. A solution may be nonmonetary; for example, terms of delivery.

- You may know more about the value of an item than the seller, so do attempt to educate them where appropriate in the interest of paying a lower price.

- Unless you have travelled somewhere for the purpose of attending an event such as an art fair, do not buy while you are on holiday. You will not be able to adequately research items and you will pay overinflated prices. It is better to buy when you have returned home.

- Do not 'badmouth' an item or say that you have seen the same thing elsewhere for a lower price in the hope of beating down the price. Keep your thoughts to yourself until after the sale is completed.

- If you are buying for the purpose of making a quick resale, do factor in purchasing costs including delivery, holding costs, selling costs and the cost of your time.

- If you are buying privately, do not show that you are interested in an item at first. Make a few bids on other items for practice. You may find a second bargain on the way to the first.

- If you are outbid at auction, do not immediately buy another item to compensate. It will not be the same. Look for opportunities at later auctions.

- Do treat the seller the way you would like to be treated.

Did you know ... Objectively examine your bargaining tools. If you come across something you cannot live without, do not walk away because you may not get a second chance. Point out damage or repairs, which will lower the value of an item.

Here are some dos and don'ts if you are the seller:

- Do shop around for the best deal if you are selling at auction, especially if you have several higher priced items to sell.

- If you are selling at auction and you expect to receive less than $75, do not put a reserve on an item. It is not worth the hassle of hanging onto it.

- At auction do set a realistic reserve such that the item sells first time. If the item is passed in, look at alternatives rather than resubmitting the item for auction. If you still wish to go to auction, review your reserve.

- Do not let yourself fall into a situation where you must sell at all costs. It is unlikely that you will get a good price.

- If you are selling privately, do remember that the potential buyer has already expended time and effort in paying you a visit, so you are in a good bargaining position. This does not apply if you are selling over the internet.

- Do sell on consignment through a dealer if you have plenty of time and want to avoid the stress of an auction. When setting a price be guided by the dealer as it is in their best interest that an item sells at a high price. Do not pay more than 20 per cent commission.

- When selling at a garage sale or street stall do remember that buyers are looking for a bargain and be prepared for some ridiculously low offers. Just laugh and do not get upset.

- Do learn as much as you can about the items you are selling so that you can set realistic prices, but bear in mind that a potential buyer may still know more about an item than you do.

- If selling over the internet, do provide accurate descriptions and good photographs.

- Do provide as much information about provenance as you can. Buyers rely on it when establishing authenticity.

- Do have a sales return policy as this is attractive to buyers. For example, allow a buyer 30 days to confirm authenticity.

- Do be upfront about condition. It is better that you are open about damage and repairs than leaving it up to the buyer to find out. They will be less likely to use it as a bargaining tool.

- Do offer discounts for multiple purchases and for payments in cash.

Generally be nice to buyers; they are a source of profit, and they are less likely to buy from you if you are grumpy. It will also make the selling experience more enjoyable.

Take precautions with any item you think might be a fake. Although it is also up to the buyer to pick this up, knowingly selling a fake as an original is fraud.

Timing

Patience is important when buying and selling collectables. A forced sale is never a good one, except by chance. When buying you need to wait for good items to come onto the market. The types of purchases you make because you cannot live without an item are not the sort of purchases that will bring good returns. Do not rush in, but do make considered choices. If you are on-selling an item, have regard to how, where and when you will resell it. Arbitrage opportunities may exist for buying at a garage sale or local market and selling at auction but they are unlikely to exist for buying and selling at two garage sales, or buying and selling online. Market mechanisms are such that prices at garage sales are generally too low and the online market is too well informed.

Publicity

Sell at well-publicised sales and auctions. If buyers do not know that your items are for sale, they cannot buy them. Buyers wish to view collectables in real life before buying them and this requires that they be on display. You can do a lot of preparatory work online but there is still no substitute for actually seeing items in person and nowhere is this more important than with collectables. Sell through dealers who are well known in your area of collecting and use auction houses that publish widely circulated catalogues. If you are selling an item for $50, you cannot expect much publicity, but if you are selling an item for $10 000, you need great publicity.

Fascinating collectables ...

Sea-shell memorabilia

Shellcraft had its origins in primitive cultures when inhabitants carved shells to use as units of currency. However, using shells to make everyday items did not take off until the reign of Queen Victoria. For many years anything made of shells was looked down upon as being pretentious and only attractive to the tourist industry. Nowadays there has been a resurgence in the market due in part to the fact that it is now illegal in many areas of Australia to remove natural materials from beaches. For example, giant clams can no longer be taken from the wild and are now worth about $3000 in good condition.

Collectable objects include mementos made by sailors at sea in the 19th century for their girlfriends at home. Examples of these items sell today at auction for thousands of dollars. Shells were also used to decorate boxes and furniture and, on a larger scale, lined the walls of English country estates. Shellcraft from this era is considered valuable. In 2009 a Victorian shellwork collage sold for more than $3500 at auction in London. Other collectable shellwork is not as expensive. A shell lei given to passengers arriving in Pacific destinations is worth around $50, which is not very much when you consider that they are rare nowadays. A vintage shell lamp from the 1950s might be worth $250.

The best-known Australian shell artists are Paul Bruce, who died in Sydney in 2008, and Bernice Standen. The value of their work varies but in the days before the global financial crisis, a larger-sized Bruce mirror surrounded by shells sold for $17 500. Standen's prices start at $185 for a small coral and barnacle cross to over $5000 for a coral and shell mirror.

Buying from overseas

If you can find the collectables you want in your own city, it is almost always best to buy them locally. For a start you will be able to personally view an item before you buy it, and secondly there are fewer potential complications with delivery. However, buying from overseas also has benefits because there is a much greater range of collectables from which to choose. Indeed some collectables may only be available overseas, while others may be much cheaper internationally, even allowing for added delivery expenses.

Following is a list of dos and don'ts when buying from overseas:

- Do check initially that Australian Customs and Quarantine allow import of the item. For example, stuffed animals may not be permitted.

- Do check that importing the item does not breach export laws in the country of origin. For example, like Australia, other countries have restrictions on the export of cultural materials.

- Do find out as much as you can about the seller. Personal references are best. If you are buying on eBay, only use sellers who have very good feedback. Use sellers who constantly deliver to Australia because they will be better informed about charges and they can tell you what to expect.

- Do pay with a secure payment medium, such as PayPal. An alternative is to use an escrow facility where payment to the seller is withheld until you have satisfactorily received the goods, but this is more difficult to organise.

- The ideal situation is for a number of overseas sellers to be offering the item you want. Do watch them and gain an idea of what a collectable is worth.

- Do not buy an item until you know the postage charges to Australia, as well as associated charges and the courier company being used. It has happened that buyers have received unexpected bills from third parties.

- Costs in addition to delivery can include import tariffs, taxes in the country of origin, GST in Australia, quarantine costs and customs handling expenses. In some cases these costs can add up to hundreds of dollars, so do know what you are up for.

- If your purchase is under cut-off limits set by the Australian government, you may not have to pay any additional charges. For example, private courier companies usually have a threshold of around $250, which means that if the value of your purchase is less than this, you do not pay additional charges. For purposes of the threshold, the figure is the declared contents value (not the purchase price) plus postage, plus an inspection fee. If using government postal services, the threshold is much higher so it may not be worth using a private courier company.

Did you know ... When buying from overseas take out insurance so that you can track the parcel and so you are covered for loss or theft.

Importing a collectable into Australia is not a straightforward process and for a purchase of a few thousand dollars you will be required to pay hefty additional charges. In addition, you may not be allowed to import some collectables at all.

Selling to overseas buyers

Because of the administration involved, if you wish to sell a collectable overseas, you are better off doing so through an auction house that has salerooms overseas, such as Christies, Sotheby's or Bonhams & Goodman. For a start, if you do it yourself, you have to ensure that you comply with the *Protection of Movable Cultural Heritage Act 1986* and the *Resale Royalty Right for Visual Artists Act 2009* (if applicable), which were covered in chapter 5. If such requirements are satisfactory, you could list your collectable on eBay in overseas countries. Remember to factor in delivery costs and foreign-exchange issues, and be prepared to respond to potential buyers who need to know the additional charges they will be up for, including such things as customs handling charges and taxes. On top of this, if you have made a practice of selling overseas, the ATO may deem you to be in business and therefore subject to income tax. The outcome is an administrative headache, which an international auction house will happily take off your hands. It can also advise you where your collectables can best be sold. In short, selling collectables overseas is best left to the experts.

Questions

When buying and selling collectables through any means, always ask questions about anything of which you are unsure. Never make assumptions about details that are not given. If you are buying or selling at a live auction, ask questions of the auction house well before the auction. You will have a further chance to do this at the start of the auction but you should know everything you need to by then. The auction is not the time to find out that payment must be made within three days if you do not have the funds available. Always ask about provenance and for a condition report.

You should never be afraid to ask obvious questions, especially if the other party is not forthright in disclosing information. Most people will answer a direct question and if they don't, look elsewhere.

If buying via the internet, ask if an item is genuine. If it turns out not to be and the seller has said that it is, you are protected by law … if you can find the seller! Ask the seller if they have any more items such as the one in question because they may be of more interest to you. This is especially true of art. Ask when delivery will be made or when you can pick an item up. Ask about insurance, which has to be arranged at the seller's end. Ask questions to establish authenticity. If selling, ask the buyer to make payment before delivery.

If you are buying stamps on eBay, be prepared to ask specific questions about their condition. This is necessary because, generally speaking, stamps available on eBay are only of 'average quality' and you will not find exceptionally good ones there. By average quality it is meant that they are worth about 25 per cent of catalogue value. Ask the seller how the stamps look. Mint or used stamps that are of catalogue value need to be fresh in all respects. They need to look about one year old if issued within 20 years, and look about five years old with a slightly aged tone (cream colour) if 50 or more years old. Condition is very important with stamps. For example, stamps with edge perforation teeth missing, or less than half-length teeth, will normally be worth only 10 per cent or less of catalogue value.

Artworks

The following is a list of dos and don'ts when buying and selling artworks. Note that artworks here include oil paintings, drawings, numbered prints, sculptures, acrylics, photographs, mixed media and new media:

- Do thoroughly research the market, as a lack of research is often quoted as the main reason for making a poor investment decision.

- When buying for profit, do not buy on impulse.

- Do not buy artworks while on holiday, unless the purpose of the trip is to attend an art fair.

- Do be wary of buying artworks at the opening of an exhibition. You will have the first look at the artwork available but you may get carried away by bubbly and emotion.

- Do be especially prudent when assessing authenticity, quality, condition and price.

- Do check the authenticity of indigenous art and major works sold on the secondary market. Only deal with a trusted source and if you have any doubts, get an independent valuation. Often indigenous art comes with a series of photographs showing the artist at work on a piece.

- Check prices closely for both the history of the work you are interested in (if any) and for similar works or other works by the same artist.

- If necessary, do talk to an art consultant who can confirm that an artwork is what it is claimed to be.

- Before buying over the internet do build trust with the particular dealers or galleries concerned, and always request the best-quality high-resolution images.

- With regard to any organisation you deal with, whether it is a gallery, dealer, auction house or consultant, do check their terms and conditions carefully as business practices vary.

If you follow these guidelines, you will give yourself the best chance of making a profit from investing in artwork.

Key points

- The first step to success in investing profitably in collectables is to do extensive research and learn about your area of speciality.

- The key determinants of value are rarity, condition and demand. Age alone does not determine rarity, although it may mean that some collectables cease to exist with the passage of time.

- Demand for a collectable in relation to its supply will have a significant effect on its value. You should seek to identify trends in demand and 'go with the flow'.

- Always seek to establish the condition of a collectable before you buy it.

- Collect items that fit your budget.

- Only buy from reputable sources. This is especially important with indigenous art.

- You are more likely to pick up a bargain at a garage sale than you are to make a profit by selling a collectable at one.

- Being considerate and courteous goes a long way when negotiating price.

- Sell at well-publicised auctions and sales.

- Think twice before you buy collectables from overseas.

- Do not be afraid to ask questions about anything you are unsure of.

- Assess authenticity, quality, condition and price when buying artworks.

10

Fraud

This chapter looks at examples of fraud that you may encounter when dealing in collectables. The incidence of fraud in this area is probably no greater than in other areas of investing activity, such as banking, finance, social security and commerce in general. One difference is that fraudulent collectables deals are usually distinguished by the nature of the schemes uncovered and often involve high-profile artists, dealers and individuals. Hence they make newsworthy stories and they are freely reported in the press. For example, social security fraud may be much more common, but the fact that someone has registered for unemployment relief under three names does not rate a mention (unless they go to jail). On the other hand, if former Wimbledon Champion John McEnroe is sold forged paintings, everyone knows about it (see 'A case of fraud' further in this chapter) because of the nature of the fraud and the profile of the person.

There is a prevalence of fakes and forgeries across a broad range of collectables, but at the outset you need to make a distinction between the two categories. A forgery of an item is a copy that has been made with a deliberate intent to defraud buyers and others, such as museums and valuers. The key attribute of a forgery is that it passed off as the 'real thing'. A fake is a copy of an item, or an alteration to one, where there may not necessarily be the intent to cover up that it is not the real thing. For example, facsimile designer watches and handbags are readily available for sale in Hong Kong for a fraction of the price of the authentic versions, but it is common knowledge that they are copies. However, forgery is illegal and so is making a fake product of a famous brand. As an investment collector you need to watch out for both because there are very good examples of fakes and forgeries that are difficult to detect, even by experts. Table 10.1 describes the incidence of fakes and forgeries for a broad cross-section of collectables.

Table 10.1: incidence of fakes and forgeries by type of collectable

Collectable	Incidence of fakes and forgeries
19th-century Australian painting: colonial and traditional	The works by leading exponents have been forged since the mid-19th century. Some artists such as Conrad Martens encouraged students to copy their work. However, the number of forged works appearing at auction and in galleries has lessened as time has gone by due to more advanced expertise and improved research technology.
Australian Impressionists	There are some fakes and forgeries.
Indigenous art	Fakes are common and they are done for the commercial market. Only buy from a reputable source.
Modern Australian painting	There are many good forgeries of works by modern artists who have since died and whose work fetched high prices at auction during the 1980s. It is more difficult to forge the work of living artists because they can authenticate their work.
Contemporary Australian art	Fakes and forgeries tend not to be a problem because most artists are still alive and they can authenticate their work.
Original prints	There are some fakes and forgeries. Be aware that an original print is a work of art. The artist alone created the master image and directed the printing. The execution of the printing and the finished print are approved by the artist, so the artist is involved at every stage. Christies International will not sell any prints by Salvador Dali printed after the 1970s because there are so many fakes on the market.

Collectable	Incidence of fakes and forgeries
British art	Galleries recognise that they have to maintain their reputations, so nowadays there tend not to be fakes and forgeries. Note that well-known, top-drawer British artwork is generally not available in Australia.
Chinese ceramics and works of art	Many copies were made in the 20th century especially of early pottery. In the 18th century it was common to copy ceramics of earlier periods and they are frequently found with earlier marks. It is important for collectors to appreciate the difference between mark and period pieces on the one hand, and pieces with marks of an earlier period on the other hand. Early artwork styles were also copied in later styles and you should be aware of this practice with regard to jade, bronze, enamel and wood carving.
Japanese art	There are not many forgeries of Meiji period pieces. Some copies have been made of Netsuke carvers with signatures added later.
Art Nouveau and Art Deco ceramics, glass, silver and works of art	Fakes and forgeries are common. Investment collectors need to be alert at all times as there are many copies on the market and they are often difficult to detect. Copies are especially common in the area of art glass, some ceramics such as those by Clarice Cliff, and certain items by such silversmiths as Georg Jensen and Josef Hoffmann.
Silver	There are few fakes. There is plenty of silver on offer in Australia that has been altered but under Australian law this is allowable. However, in the UK the same alterations render silver illegal to be sold unless each alteration is hallmarked, so check whether your altered silver has been hallmarked if you plan to sell it in the UK.
Australian jewels	None known
Australian glass	None known
English and European glass	In the 19th and 20th centuries it was common to add wheel engravings to 18th-century glass. This is difficult to detect. There are some forgeries, especially of Continental glass.
Antiquities	An almost infinite list of fakes and forgeries, many made in the 19th century and up to the 1940s. They are difficult to detect in sculpture.

Table 10.1 (*cont'd*): incidence of fakes and forgeries by type of collectable

Collectable	Incidence of fakes and forgeries
Islamic rugs, pottery, metalwork and ivory	There are some forgeries. A lot of pottery is fake.
Australian colonial furniture	Only a few. Some signed pieces are suspected of having the maker's name added afterwards. There are some fakes of depression-era furniture.
English and Continental furniture	There are numerous 19th-century copies of 18th-century pieces. There are also many altered pieces.
English and Continental pottery and porcelain	There are forgeries of both. There was a lot of copying of both in Paris in the 19th century, which is relatively easy to detect. There are some outright fakes and forgeries.
Coins and medals	There are examples of fakes and forgeries on the market. In particular, there have been forgeries of the Holey Dollar made in Asia.
Stamps	Every issue of British stamps since about the time they were first introduced in the 1860s has been forged because people wanted to evade paying postage. Note that some forgeries have a higher value than the original issue. Prior to 1910, each Australian state had its own stamps and forgeries were fairly common. Commonwealth stamps were first produced in 1913 and forgeries became less common because so much fame had been given to forgeries that people were more aware of them.
Books	You must be careful because facsimile copies do exist.
Cars: automobilia	Few veteran or vintage cars are completely original. They may range from having some parts replaced to having everything new except the chassis. There is a good deal of changing of engine numbers. More recent classic cars are easy to replicate. A GTO Falcon or a Mustang is easy to forge.
Rock-and-roll memorabilia	There are few fakes and forgeries but beware of gold discs, which are a major problem. Many autographs of the most popular stars of the 1950s and 1960s are fakes signed by managers, road crew and general staff. Unless a piece of memorabilia is obviously genuine, it should come with authentication.

It is important to be aware of the characteristics of fakes and forgeries in your area of collecting as they may be difficult to tell apart from the originals and you can be seriously misled.

The likelihood that you will be sold a fake or a forged item is one of the biggest problems you will face with investment collecting. For example, Professor Charles Stannish of UCLA in Los Angeles was quoted in the May–June 2009 issue of *Archeology* as saying that 95 per cent of antiquities for sale on eBay were fakes. This was up from 50 per cent in 1995. Stannish also claims that fake artefacts and scams are so advanced on eBay that even the experts cannot determine what is genuine.

These findings by Professor Stannish have to be treated with caution because his comments relate to US artefacts, such as Native American arrowheads and Neolithic tooth pendants, and he was not referring to all collectables. Nevertheless, he found that extremely good fake artefacts were being mass produced nowadays and one of the results of this was that the values of genuine artefacts had declined.

Intent to defraud

Forgery and making a fake of a branded item are considered illegal in Australia. However, the seller of a collectable is only guilty of a criminal offence if they know that the item is a fake or forgery and they intend that others believe that it is genuine. This may be difficult to prove and a court may indeed not make a ruling on this offence but may instead rule that the seller make restitution to others, including the maker of the collectable.

For example, in mid 2010 a case was decided in the Victorian Supreme Court where it was held that three drawings by Charles Blackman and Robert Dickerson were fakes, but the presiding judge made no finding as to whether the owner knew them to be fakes. The drawings in question were *Street Scene with Schoolgirl* and *Three Schoolgirls* by Charles Blackman and *Pensive Woman* by Robert Dickerson. Blackman and Dickerson brought an action against a Melbourne gallery owner and valuer of the three artworks. In a long-running case, Justice Vickery said the drawings 'were fakes masquerading as the genuine article. What is more, they were deliberately contrived to deceive unsuspecting members of the public in this manner ... The false signatures drawn on each of the works could have had no other purpose'. The judge ordered the destruction of the fakes and gave the gallery owner 30 days to appeal. After that the drawings were to be delivered to Blackman and Dickerson, who had to destroy them within seven days.

The gallery owner did not appeal and Blackman, Dickerson and others burned the fakes in a celebratory bonfire in Sydney in July 2010 bringing the matter to an end.

A case of fraud

A common fraudulent practice with collectables is for an intermediary, such as a dishonest dealer, to sell the same piece to unsuspecting buyers more than once or to sell pieces they have never owned in the first place. When it comes time to make delivery, the intermediary disappears. This ruse can sometimes be carried out on a large scale, but note that for every case that is prosecuted other offenders get away with it. Other instances of fraud revolve around the misdealings of intermediaries where the underlying collectables exist but where they are fraudulently used.

In April 2010 Lawrence Salander, a New York art dealer, received a hefty fine and up to 18 years in jail for defrauding 30 clients of US$120 million between 2004 and 2007. His clients included former US tennis star John McEnroe, who lost US$2 million when Salander sold him two pieces he fraudulently claimed were by Archie Gorky, a US artist of Armenian origin.

Other victims included Robert De Niro Sr, father of Hollywood actor Robert De Niro, and the mother of Beastie Boys musician, Michael Diamond. De Niro entrusted Salander to be the sole dealer of the works belonging to his father, but in 2007 Salander sold two De Niro paintings to an unnamed third party for US$77 000 and had the entire amount paid directly into the personal bank account of his gallery director without saying anything to De Niro.

With the profits he made, Salander bought a luxurious Manhattan residence and a private aeroplane. He was ordered to repay the US$120 million to his clients. The Manhattan District Attorney said that Salander's 'widespread fraud and calculated betrayal created ripples that spread from individual victims to the broader art world'.

Guidelines for selecting genuine collectables

No-one is an expert on everything so you cannot be expected to know all the 'tips and traps' for picking up fakes and forgeries. However, whether your speciality is stamps, books, coins, real crystal, autographs, militaria, model cars, Murano glass, silverware, paintings, sculpture, textiles or uranium glass, there is usually a way of telling whether a collectable is genuine. The range of collectables is too vast to cover each one of them in this book, so the following is a summary of guidelines for detecting fakes and forgeries and for avoiding being defrauded.

Price

If something looks too good to be true, it probably is. If, for example, someone is offering you an Australian 1930 penny in extremely fine condition for $5000 instead of the market price of $50 000, it is either a forgery or there is something wrong with it. However, the onus is on you to have a ballpark idea of what something is worth in the first place. Similarly, if you are offered a painting by a prominent artist at a vastly reduced price, you may not have any doubt that the painting itself is real, but first check that the seller has good title to it.

The price should be a general indicator of whether an item is genuine or not. The exception is if a seller has no knowledge of what they are selling or does not care about its value. For example, some years ago on eBay in the UK a woman sold her partner's expensive sports car for US$0.50 because she had heard him flirting with a model he had heard on the radio. However, in the general scheme of things, a starting price of $0.99 on eBay for a big brand name item is suspect. A cheap price usually equates with cheap quality, but it may be that the seller does not know what they are selling, or that you are just the lucky buyer stumbling across a bargain.

Fascinating collectables ...

Early Australian jazz vinyl records

Collecting vinyl records is a popular hobby and one that is not very expensive. Even rare and sought-after records may be purchased for less than $100. Some hallmark records cost more, but others of collectable quality cost as little as $5 to $10. One genre is early Australian jazz, which includes records by Graeme Bell, Bob and Len Barnard, Dave Dallwitz, Frank Johnson, Smacka Fitzgibbon, The Red Onions Jazz Band and John Sangster. The genre had its origins in Melbourne in the 1950s and early 1960s, and record labels included Swaggie, Crest Records, W&G and Magnasound. Swaggie, founded by Graeme Bell and Nevill L Sherburn, was the most important label and it released around 300 records. Bell was a friend of Sidney Nolan, who supplied the artwork for *The Ned Kelly Suite*, which is worth up to $100, but the value of a typical Swaggie record today in good condition is only $20 to $30. You can get cheaper records on eBay but the condition may be dubious.

More modern jazz records are also sought after by collectors. In 1958 The Australian All Stars band was formed featuring Don Burrows and they released two LPs called *Jazz for Beachniks*. These albums are considered rare, but even more scarce is an original copy of an album released in 1967 by the Charlie Munro Quartet called *Eastern Horizons*. Similarly rare are *Psychedelia Part 3* by Graeme Lyall, *Downunder Blues* by Georgia Lee and a complete set of the four-part *Lord of the Rings* series by John Sangster. Regardless of the fact that these albums have been re-released on CD, the original records are still valuable.

Sellers

Ask the seller straight out if an item is genuine. For example, 'Is this item genuine crystal? Does it have a sticker? Where was it made?' If you are checking crystal in person, give the piece a flick with your finger nail; it should make a pinging sound. If it is glass, it will make a clunk. Glass can be made to look like crystal, so always use the finger-nail test. If you cannot get satisfactory answers from the seller, do not buy the item.

Only deal with reputable sellers. On eBay you can check a seller's feedback ratings, but always beware of buying valuable collectables online because you will usually need an opportunity to see them first in person. Wherever possible buy from reputable dealers, auction houses and galleries, especially in the case of collectables such as indigenous art.

One of the things you can do if you suspect a fishy deal is to ask the seller how and where they acquired an item and for what price. You might not get straight answers but you should be able to get an idea of their credibility.

Read the fine print

Look for a maker's mark. Most genuine items of good repute have a maker's mark of some sort. A maker's mark is some mark, initials, design, sticker or tag that indicates that an item was made by a particular person or in a particular factory. Sometimes, due to age or other factors, the maker's mark, tag or sticker has been removed or lost. China and porcelain are the most famous examples of items with makers' marks. With china, a maker's mark can sometimes be traced back hundreds or even thousands of years. The maker's mark denotes both the maker and the era in which the china was made. Unmarked china and porcelain are very common, but the most famous and valuable pieces will always have a maker's mark that can be fairly easily identified. Another item that has a maker's mark is sterling or solid silver, which has a hallmark indicating where and when it was made. If an item has a hallmark, it will be genuine silver rather than plated. Silver that is marked E.P.N.S. or E.A. is plated and not as valuable.

If you are reading an item description, for example, in a written catalogue or on eBay, check all of the details carefully and look for clues that an item is not what it appears to be. For example, look out for words or phrases such as 'style', 'similar to', 'copy', 'approximately', 'in the style of', 'era', 'circa' and 'repro'. If the word 'vintage' is used, make sure that the collectable is indeed vintage and that it does not just have the 'look' of being old.

Use your own eyes

When it comes to buying collectables, personal inspection beforehand is always preferable. You can assess such things as size, authenticity and condition much better in real life. You know that if an item does not meet your expectations, or if you are still in doubt when you see it, you do not have to buy it. You can take someone with you, such as a dealer, who can provide an expert opinion that the item is genuine and who can provide an estimate of value. Failing a personal inspection, the next best thing is that you buy an item on a sale or return basis. If you have, say, 30 days to make up your mind, you can carry out all the checks you would have done at an inspection and indeed more. For example, you can see whether an item fits with your surroundings.

Examine the quality of an object. This is difficult to do unless you see it in person, but if you are buying online you can compare different descriptions. In the flesh, handle an item and use the knowledge you have acquired through research. For example, if you are considering buying a Murano glass vase, it should be weighty and thick and the colour should be bright. The design should be clever, inventive and beautiful, and you need to be able to distinguish it from vases sold at The Reject Shop.

Did you know ... Use your knowledge and experience when viewing collectables and assessing prospective offers. Politely ask the other party to substantiate their claims.

Do your homework. Do not be left wondering if you are really getting a bargain. You need to familiarise yourself with all the details of an item, including styles, features and colours, and with regard to collectables, availability. If an item is only rarely made available for sale, you need to know that. Check the provenance of artwork and such clues as a certificate of authenticity, receipts or guarantees from the previous owner, and a sticker or stamp on the reverse of a painting saying where or when it was framed. Check the signature on paintings and make sure that a painting is not really a print that has been printed onto textured canvas, which can look quite believable.

Follow your instincts. If you do not feel right about buying the antique pocket watch you are thinking about, do not do it. There will be other opportunities, so keep looking. The same applies to any deal that you are unsure about. It is better to be safe than to be taken for a ride.

eBay and fraud

In the US alone eBay spends US$20 million a year trying to prevent fraud. Nevertheless, it has had to fight lawsuits over fake items for some years. For example, in April 2010 a US Federal Appeals Court upheld a lower court ruling that eBay was not liable for fake Tiffany trinkets being sold on its website. As part of a concerted effort to crack down on fraud, eBay's Security and Resolution Centre in the US lists a number of precautions that buyers should take to prevent being defrauded. These include the following guidelines:

- Learn as much as possible about the seller and the item being sold. Check all of the facts and check feedback scores and look for positive reviews.

- Check return and refund polices. Reputable sellers are not afraid to offer guarantees.

- Research items ahead of time. Look for availability, professional valuations and prices. If something is being sold cheaply, there is usually a reason for it.

- Research the seller's past sales. Pay particular attention to similar items that have been sold. Note that collectables do not come in bulk.

- Obtain professional alternative opinions on expensive items.

- Use PayPal instead of a credit card, bank transfer or money order because PayPal offers recourse for reimbursement.

- Assess the seller's knowledge about an item. A reputable seller will be able to provide answers to most of your questions.

- Request additional photographs. If a seller claims to have certificates of authenticity, ensure that they are from a reputable source.

Did you know ...

If you have any doubts about a transaction, walk away from it. There will always be other opportunities worth seeking.

Basically you should take a commonsense approach when seeking to avoid fraud. Be realistic about the price of an item and be on guard if it seems artificially low. Aim to be as knowledgeable as the seller about any item you are interested in. Do not take anything at face value and bring up any concerns that you have.

Common forgeries and fakes to watch out for

All types of collectables have features that distinguish an original item from a fake or forgery. It may be as specific as the style of a maker's mark or the way an artist signs paintings, or perhaps there are signs that an item came into existence at a time after the original was produced. Whatever these signs may be, it is up to you as an investment collector to know what they are in regard to your speciality. You can learn from the experience of others, especially experts and experienced collectors, but bear in mind that even experts can be fooled. In this section we explain what to look out for when assessing vintage art pottery, vintage costume jewellery and militaria.

Fraud and vintage art pottery

Depending on the type of collectable you are interested in, there are steps you can take to ensure that you are not being sold an imperfect item. For example, many fake and restored pieces of vintage art pottery are being sold nowadays in 'mint' condition, so you need to be aware of what to look out for when adding to your investment collection. Vintage art pottery may have chips or a crack, or some of the glaze or gilding may have worn away. These flaws are all repairable and to the untrained eye the restoration may not be noticeable. An honest dealer or seller will designate a piece as 'restored' but not everyone is honest. When buying vintage art pottery, follow these guidelines:

- Always ask at the beginning of an inspection whether a piece has been restored. If the seller is evasive, do not buy the piece.

- A restored piece will have slight variations in colour hue, which can be detected with an ultraviolet light. You should check this before making an expensive purchase.

- If you suspect that a handle or other part of a piece has been added to an item through restoration, tap the suspect part with a coin. If it is indeed a restoration, there will be a slightly different sound compared with when you tap the main body of the piece.

- Restored art pottery should be cheaper than a piece in true mint condition.

Note also the maker's mark, which is on the underside of vintage art pottery. These are a key determinant of value, but they can be removed or changed or added to, and this is especially so of makers' marks that are printed rather then impressed. When buying vintage art pottery in higher price brackets it is always a good idea to scrutinise the piece for mark tampering. However, you are not as likely to see this on pieces at the lower end of the market.

Did you know ...

To ensure that a maker's mark is original, study the glazing underneath the item to determine if it is consistent, with no signs of scraping or filling.

Today there are many examples of reproduced vintage art pottery on the market. Many pieces aimed at the high end of the market are being reproduced in China and sold as original art pottery from various potters, some of which have been out of business for 20 years or more. Fakes from Asia tend to show poor workmanship, being made from substandard moulds, with poor glazes. An expert or astute collector can easily spot these fakes, but someone with an untrained eye cannot, so when buying a piece your first question should be: 'Is this a reproduction?' This is especially the case if you are buying online.

Unglazed art pottery is generally easier to reproduce and examples are commonplace. Moulds are taken from the original pieces and reproduced into modern ceramics. However, often a potter who made originals back in the 1920s, 1930s and 1940s has simply taken their old moulds and reproduced and reissued collectables in modern times. This practice has created valuation issues for dealers and collectors alike when looking at a potter's work as a whole. Original pieces tend to be more refined with clearer detail because the earlier potters took more time to finish and perfect a piece before it was fired.

There has been a revival of vintage art pottery, but pieces can be expensive. Knowing what to look for is important because there are many fakes on the market. To build an investment collection, start with one piece and then add more by the same maker.

Fraud and vintage costume jewellery

Vintage costume jewellery is another area where there are many fakes masquerading as the real thing. Pieces may be signed or unsigned and it may be difficult to tell what is genuine and what is not. Protect and educate yourself by reading books, speaking to experts and researching trusted websites, and familiarise yourself with designs, colour combinations and signatures. It is also useful to learn how particular designers made their pieces because it will enable you to detect a fake quickly. For example, if a particular designer was known for prong setting gemstones in their jewellery and you encountered a piece where a stone was glued, you would know that it was a fake.

Go to antique shows and get to know dealers, who are often happy to share their knowledge with new collectors. Research dealers as well as designers, and only trade with reputable ones. Dealers may sell fakes but they may not do it on purpose, so only do business with established dealers with good reputations. If buying online, do everything possible to protect yourself. Make sure that sellers have a good return policy and if using an internet auction site such as eBay, ensure that a seller has received plenty of positive feedback.

With vintage costume jewellery fakes exist at both the high and low ends of the market, but it is more common to see them at the higher end. If you are not familiar with vintage costume jewellery, and you do not yet have a trained eye, avoid buying expensive pieces.

It is not uncommon for a fake to be vintage itself, as many were created around the same time as the original pieces. If you like the look of a vintage fake piece and you are not concerned about provenance, it makes a good purchase, but do not buy it for investment purposes. Many of the companies that made vintage fakes are no longer in business, so there is little concern about supporting fraudulent practices. However, for anyone who is an investment collector and who values the craftsmanship of designer vintage pieces, you need to be cautious.

Sellers of vintage costume jewellery need to be knowledgeable about fakes as well. It is bad to unknowingly buy a fake, but it is even worse to unknowingly sell one. As a seller, you need to be educated and informed about all the pieces you are selling. It is important to protect buyers and your reputation.

Fraud and militaria

There is an ever-growing number of fake medals, swords, bayonets, uniforms, helmets and other items of militaria on the market today and unsuspecting buyers pay high prices for them. For example, an Australian Special Air Services (SAS) beret made in China sold on eBay for over $300. For a collector, one of the attractions of a genuine beret is that it was worn by an SAS soldier, but obviously that is not the case with a fake and it is worth little to someone who is aware. The numbers of fake militaria are a huge problem in the market. Reasons for the prevalence of fakes in this area include the following:

- Militaria is becoming more rare with the passage of time as the number of original items of military value are disappearing due to theft, house fires, disasters, and wear and tear. Hence, supply is dwindling.

• Wealthy collectors have arrived on the market and they are scooping up large numbers of items of value. Supply is dwindling for this reason also.

• The advent of mass production technology means that fakes can be made in countries such as China and India at the rate of hundreds per day at very low cost.

• A lot of militaria is sold on eBay and the company's resources preclude it from policing sales to the extent that collectors would like.

The circumstances just described have created an environment that enables the makers and sellers of fakes to generate substantial profits. If you are using eBay to make a purchase, the first thing you should do is check the search listings as there are often many sellers offering the same item. Once you have found the item you are interested in, compare the sellers' listings. If there are differences in what each seller is offering, try and work out which sounds more credible and reliable. Next check photographs and item descriptions. A good photograph will reveal peculiarities of an original item, including age, wear and tear, maker's mark, silver and gold grades, broken and damaged pieces, size and condition. These clues will help you assess the item's authenticity.

Did you know ...

Some sellers have been known to age an item artificially, but most find this to be too time consuming and ultimately do not bother.

Age matters, and it shows up in even the best-conditioned pieces. It is an absolute indicator of authenticity. If you have to assess age, or any other factor, from a photograph and its quality is unclear, ask for another photo. The item's description should clearly state whether it is original or not; there is no valid reason for not addressing this issue. A full statement of authenticity is desirable, as is a money back guarantee.

There are many good books and price guides available on militaria and you have the opportunity to be knowledgeable. Also join clubs and associations; among other things you will find out which sellers are reputable. By reading books about the items you are interested in, and studying and handling them at fairs and auctions, you will derive a great deal of understanding. You will also create a working knowledge of the originals and be less likely to be defrauded.

Key points

- You need to distinguish between a 'forgery' on one hand and a 'fake' on the other. A forgery is a copy that has been made with the deliberate intent to defraud. A fake is a copy that is not necessarily made dishonestly.

- The reason for the existence of forgeries and fakes is that the perpetrators wish to make money. There would not be forgeries and fakes if there was no demand for the originals.

- There is a varying prevalence of forgeries and fakes across a broad range of collectables. As an investment collector you need to be cautious.

- Some forgeries and fakes are so good that even experts have difficulty detecting them.

- If a deal looks too good to be true, it probably is.

- Many collectables have a maker's mark, which is one of the first things you should look for. Note that a mark may be added later or altered or removed.

- Sometimes a forgery of an item is more valuable than the original; for example, early British postage stamps.

- Vintage fakes exist in some areas of collecting, which means that they are as old as the originals as they were produced at the same time.

- Always research an item carefully before you buy it. If you are selling an item, make sure that it is genuine in order to protect the buyer and your reputation.

- There is no substitute for a personal inspection of an item before you buy. Take an expert with you if you wish to confirm an item's value. This may cost you a small fee but it is worth it for expensive items.

- Vintage art pottery, vintage costume jewellery and militaria are three areas of collecting where fakes are common and often hard to detect.

11

How to make money from investing in collectables

To make money from investing in collectables you need to treat it like a rational profit-making venture. Over your time horizon, which could be five to 10 years, you need to generate more revenue than you pay out in expenses, including tax. However, just making a profit is not enough because your returns need to be better than the rate of inflation and you have to consider the opportunity cost as well — that is, your money could have been invested elsewhere and making similar or much better returns.

For example, if you have an alternative investment proposal that will return you 8 per cent per annum before tax, then investing in collectables has to generate at least the same return to make it worthwhile. For the purposes of this chapter, the potential non-monetary benefits you can derive from investing in collectables are disregarded and instead we review the main points you need to know to make collectables work as a profitable investment.

Basically, if you are going to buy collectables as an investment, you should:

1 buy something that interests you

2 choose collectables with highly liquid markets

3 reduce your holding costs by buying collectables that do not need special treatment or do not need to be kept in special conditions

4 set yourself a time limit—for example, if the collectable has not increased in value after five years, consider selling it.

Follow your interests

Focus on your interests when selecting collectables in which to invest as making a profit will be far more enjoyable. If you buy collectables that you are interested in, you are more likely to become an expert in your field. If you attempt to invest in an area that doesn't appeal to you, it will become a chore and you will not buy and sell well. The time you spend improving your knowledge of a type of collectable will pay off because you will develop the skills necessary to assess true worth and make money. And if you are not interested in collectables, look elsewhere for investment opportunities. This cannot be emphasised too strongly.

Liquidity

Collectables are often illiquid investments and you may be unable to get your money back when you want to, even at a reduced price. It is true that property may take months to sell, but collectables can take years. On the other hand, shares and bonds can always be sold on financial markets and you receive your money in three days—although you might not always obtain the price you would like.

Always consider how easily you can sell your collectables without being forced to make a distressed sale. Collectables, especially obscure ones, are often thinly traded or not traded at all and markets may be nonexistent. Also, there are often wide movements in the desirability of certain collectables. For example, these days discreet types of collecting, such as stamps, coins and banknotes, have given way to more decorative elements used for outward display. Another factor is that each sector has different levels of difficulty for the would-be investment collector and collectables where markets are illiquid can be extremely difficult to master.

Did you know …

Factor in the liquidity of a collectable's market when thinking about whether to invest. You will want to be able to buy and sell as easily as possible, even though they are usually long-term investments.

Unless you choose to collect something that is out of the realm of mainstream collectables (and this is not recommended if you wish to make money) make sure you establish that a liquid market exists for your area of specialisation—that is, a market where there are usually numerous buyers and sellers. Otherwise you will encounter serious problems if you need to sell quickly. You may not buy with the intention of selling soon afterwards, but unforeseen circumstances may compel you to dispose of your purchases before you otherwise would.

If you have an eye on profit when selecting an area of collectables in which to invest, focus on ones that appeal to dealers and auction houses because this helps to ensure liquidity.

Ease of management

When assessing ease of management, consider whether you will need to spend money to keep the collectable in special conditions. Nowadays, apartments and houses are generally drier, creating problems with many natural materials, such as wood or ivory. On the other hand, dryness is beneficial for paper and metals.

The cost of special conservation measures—referred to in the industry as preventative conservation—such as humidifiers and wine cabinets, may affect the popularity and market strength of the collectables needing them. Additional security systems can also add to the expense of a collection. Broad markets with many collectors make it easier for thieves to sell stolen goods. For example, stamps are easier to sell than a Picasso painting, although Picassos get stolen, too. Check the Stolen Paintings Record before you purchase an expensive European painting.

Generally speaking, the more valuable a collection, the greater is the need for security. Also the greater the need for adequate insurance, which can add substantially to the costs of maintaining a collection.

Time horizon

Some collectables, such as jewellery, first day covers, wine, stamps, vases and coins, may take many years to appreciate in value. Other areas, such as paintings and prints by well-known artists and indigenous art, can appreciate more quickly. The area you choose to specialise in will partly be determined by how quickly you aim to make a profit, bearing in mind that there is no such thing as a guaranteed return. Many investors have found to their regret that the value of their collection depreciates rather than appreciates.

When you buy a collectable, set a time frame for holding it and review your investment at the end of this period. The time limit will vary from purchase to purchase but three to five years may be taken as a general guide. The important thing is that you have a time in mind during which the collectable should appreciate in value. If an investment has not met your expectations, sell it and buy something else. A regular review forces you to prune out losing collectables in the same way you would sell dud shares.

Did you know ... Although you might not know for many years whether you are making a profit on a purchase, have a time frame in mind, rather than let an investment continue indefinitely.

Fascinating collectables ...

Early television sets

Television in Australia was launched in September 1956 and there have been collectors of sets ever since. However, they are bulky items and they take up a lot of space so they have never caught on in the same way as collecting radios. Today there are very few televisions left of the sort that were in use in 1956 and one in good condition is worth around $500, but the early models were heavy, which acts as a deterrent to collecting them. In the early 1960s home-theatre-style television sets were popular. These combined a television set, a radio and a hi-fi record player, and again they were bulky and heavy. However, they are collectable and in good condition they sell for $200 to $300, or less if you agree to pick them up.

Today the most collectable television set is the JVC Video-sphere (model 3240), which is a small nine-inch set that was produced in the early 1970s. They are particularly collectable because their design was so distinctive (like an astronaut's helmet according to some observers). Also they could run on batteries, so were suitable for boats and cars, and some models had a clock. These sets came in orange, ivory, white, grey and black, which is considered the rarest. Their estimated value is $300 to $400 depending on condition and colour. The first portable television sets from the 1980s are now coming to be considered collectable and they are currently worth about $25.

If you are collecting televisions, it is always preferable that they are in working order. When digital television is Australia-wide you will need a converter to make them workable.

Investment strategy

You need a well put together strategic plan when investing in collectables, the same as you do with any other profit-making venture. Otherwise you will end up with an investment portfolio that is unbalanced and likely to be filled with collectables simply because they were available, rather than because they fit into your overall strategy. In formulating an investment strategy you need to decide what percentage of your overall wealth you will invest in collectables.

Diversification

It is important to diversify your investment portfolio and not 'put all your eggs in one basket'. Hence you should not have an investment portfolio made up solely of collectables. For a start, collectables usually do not generate an income stream so they do not provide any revenue until you sell them—and this could be years away. In addition, collectables cost money to insure and in some cases just to conserve. They cannot usually be regarded as 'safe' investments as their value will not necessarily rise and may even fall—just like any other investment.

The markets for collectables are never as well defined as they are for conventional financial products as each collectable is unique. Each collectable's quality and condition will vary, and so will their values. It is recommended that you allocate 5 per cent to 10 per cent of your investment portfolio to collectables, so if you have $100000 to invest, you would earmark $5000 to $10000 for them. This would automatically rule out some collectables, such as classic cars, and more expensive artwork, unless you are wealthy. On the other hand, it costs little to invest in mint proof coins, autographed books, first day covers or entertainment show programs.

Diversification within categories of collectables

In developing an investment strategy you also need to consider diversifying your collectables portfolio within categories of collectables. You might choose to invest in emerging Australian artists, but here again it would be most unwise to put all your eggs in one basket, so have a spread of artists, time periods and genres. Alternatively, you can opt for a balanced portfolio of collectables and buy stamps, coins, art, furniture and antiques, books and jewellery. If one area performs badly, you have the other areas to fall back on as it is unlikely that all categories would fall in value simultaneously. But this does mean that you will spend more time on your collectables as you will need to keep up to date in many different areas.

Risk

You investment strategy will also need to address risk. When assessing risk, the first thing you will need to be concerned with is the length of time the market for your collectables has been established. New markets, such as contemporary art, may fluctuate widely according to availability and whether the particular painter is in or out of fashion. When trying to minimise risk, consider whether or not there is a substantial body of background information. An area of collectables that is well covered by easily obtainable reference work, including books and specialist magazines, will generally be more assessable because the collector has knowledgeable references to consult.

Did you know …

An element of risk is present in all investments. Your aim is to minimise it by completing thorough research, developing skills in buying and selling, and by setting a limit to how much you will invest.

As with any profit-making venture, do not invest more than you can afford to lose. You will have to confront the possibility of significant loss from your investing activities at times, so have contingency plans in place. For example, if you have invested in Victorian furniture, consider selling your current holdings and taking a loss and invest in a new area of collectables.

Potential return

Make sure you have a general idea of the return you can expect from investing in collectables. This is difficult with collectables that go in and out of fashion, such as wallpaper, but more reliable estimates are available for such collectables as stamps, coins, banknotes, wine and the artworks of established artists. For the collectables that can either generate spectacular returns or losses, such as the artworks of emerging artists, mitigate your potential loss by earmarking investments as 'speculation' and do not overload your portfolio with them.

When assessing your potential return, consider the stability of the market and the degree to which prices fluctuate. While the prices of some items, such as furniture, remain relatively stable, others such as tribal art move erratically in and out of favour. Note whether your type of collectable attracts buyers in many countries because this makes for stable markets and it might compensate for currency fluctuations. For example, if foreign currencies are strong against the Australian dollar, expatriate buyers will fill a gap left by Australians at home. In Australia, there will always be a high demand for Australian art.

Specific types of collectables, such as famous paintings or rare books, will tend to increase in value more quickly than more widely held collectables, such as wine, coins, stamps and comic books. It is essential to develop an eye for what to collect and for which items are likely to increase in value the fastest. The first step in this process is to select an area that appeals to you from a profit-making viewpoint and then to research it thoroughly.

Quality versus quantity

It has been emphasised throughout this book that quality takes precedence over quantity and that you should buy the best collectables you can afford. This is true because high-quality items will appreciate more in value and because they are easier to sell in good times and in bad. However, this rule is subject to a few qualifications. Firstly, it generally does not make sense to spend time saving for a few years to buy one piece and then wait and save for a few more years to buy another one. If you follow this pattern, you will not qualify as an investment collector.

Secondly, if you have good reason to expect a collectable to take off overnight, you might want to aim for a quick killing, even though the collectable is not of top quality. For purposes of speculation, you might not buy 'quality over quantity', but note that speculating is a high risk activity, and as such it may not fit your overall investment strategy.

Thirdly, if your circumstances are such that you cannot wait five to 10 years for a collectable to appreciate because you need an income stream in the meantime, there are a couple of things you can do. One of these is to focus on the art rental market, where you can earn 8 per cent per annum pre-tax or higher if you negatively gear your investment. Another thing you can do is buy numerous lower quality collectables with the intention of selling them off piecemeal in the coming years. If you only have one high quality collectable and you need money, you would have to sell the entire piece, but if you have several lower value pieces, you would only need to sell off one or two.

Did you know ... There is always a trade-off between quality and quantity. As a guide buy the best you can afford, but make allowances for the possible need to sell off collectables to enhance your liquidity.

Transaction costs

The transaction costs associated with buying and selling collectables are significantly higher than those associated with other forms of investing, such as bonds and shares. They are also significantly higher than property investments. Depending on what you buy and how you buy it, you may be liable for a commission of 10 per cent or more on both the buying and selling price. Dealers' mark-ups are 33 to 50 per cent or more. This compares with buying and selling shares where commissions can be as low as 0.15 per cent. When buying property there are legal costs but no agents' commissions. When selling property the agents' commissions are around 2 per cent.

There may be additional costs associated with security, insurance and caring for your collectables. While an investment property carries with it similar charges, there are no such costs attached to investing in shares and bonds. If you are renting out collectables, you can claim a tax deduction for property-related expenses as you are generating rental income.

Information

Choose to invest in areas of collectables that have good sources of information available because you will need them as a guide for your sound financial decisions. The markets for collectables are not as well documented as they are for shares, bonds and property, so you will need to develop research skills. As discussed in 'Useful resources' at the end of this book much of this information costs money, whereas information on other investment markets is freely available in newspapers and on the internet.

Books about collectables broadly fall into two categories: those that deal with particular collectables (for example golf clubs) and price guides. There are none that tell you how to make money.

Rarity

Generally invest in collectables that show a propensity to becoming scarce as rarity is often the key determinant of value. Find out how rare an item or piece is before you buy it and research the likelihood that it will become scarcer. For example, active living artists can paint additional works, while the market is finite with deceased artists.

Location matters

Most major dealers and auction houses are located in the main cities in Australia, especially Melbourne and Sydney. This is a limiting factor when it comes to buying and selling some collectables. While it is often possible to bid at auctions by telephone or online and you do not need to be present to sell at auction, it is easier to do both in person. Also, as we mention throughout this book, there is no substitute for a personal inspection of an item before you buy it. It is because of this that buying and selling collectables online has not been a great success.

To buy collectables with real confidence you need to examine them yourself at a dealer's shop—a dealer themselves would never buy an item without seeing it first. In addition, individual buyers and sellers are located in cities rather than outlying areas. For these reasons close proximity to major cities can be a determining factor in your choice of collectables.

Location is not such an issue with other investment types. While the markets for collectables are fragmented according to where you live, the markets for shares and bonds are uniform across Australia. If you are selling shares or bonds, you are quoted the same price no matter where you are based.

Did you know … When dealing in collectables it is usually an advantage to be located in or near a major city. One exception is country auctions, where bargains are often there to be had.

With regard to buying and selling internationally, generally speaking if you buy collectables from overseas, you will have to sell them overseas if you want the best price. This is especially true of expensive collectables, such as European art. In this case you need to factor in foreign currency fluctuations.

If you can find the collectables you want in your city, it is almost always best to buy them locally. For a start you will be able to personally view an item before you buy it, and secondly there are fewer potential complications with delivery. However, buying from overseas has benefits because there is a much greater range of collectables from which to choose. Indeed some collectables may only be available overseas, while others may be much cheaper to buy from there even after factoring in additional delivery expenses. Selling collectables overseas is best left to the experts.

Valuations

When you invest in collectables it is not possible to know for sure what they are worth to you until you sell them. You can seek a professional valuation but even then there is no guarantee of accuracy. Sometimes a valuation might be done for insurance purposes and then when the item is sold at auction the price it actually brings could be vastly different, depending on the day. As noted in chapter 7, the price of a seemingly identical item could be very different from the one you own due to such things as condition or attribution. The profits or losses you make from investing in collectables cannot be determined until you sell them and that may be many years into the future.

Condition

There is always the possibility that a collectable will become damaged, which will obviously not be an issue with shares and bonds. Property can be damaged but repairs of that kind are much more desirable than repairs to collectables. The condition of collectables is important both when you are considering buying them and when you are faced with maintaining their condition.

Physical ownership

When investing in collectables it is generally preferable to have physical ownership of the assets rather than to own securities over companies that trade in the particular collectables, as you will make more money. In times of economic uncertainty the price of gold increases and at present it is at record high levels. Hence the value of gold jewellery and gold bullion coins has also increased.

This prompts the question: are you better off investing in a gold-mining company or in a collectable that has a gold component, such as a gold bullion coin? The answer is that you are better off investing in a gold-mining company because you derive greater leverage. For example, if you bought gold today at, say, US$1400 per ounce to get a 10 per cent gain, you would need the price to increase to US$1540. On the other hand, if you bought a gold share for A$1, you only need it to rise to A$1.10. Also, if you are buying shares in a gold-mining company that is producing 50 000 ounces of gold, you have much greater leverage over the gold price.

The value of rare gold coins such as the sovereign is more determined by the rarity, condition and demand for the coins, rather than for their gold content. The same is true of vintage gold jewellery but modern jewellery may be bought for its gold content. Gold bullion coins and modern gold jewellery are two areas where you may wish to cash in on an increasing gold price.

Lifestyle

Focus on collecting items that are appropriate to your lifestyle. Many people base their collections on their hobbies, such as collecting tin soldiers, but it does not make sense to collect wine, for example, if you do not have the space and environment to store it properly or the inclination to monitor its progress.

Fraud

You need to be aware of fraud both with regard to being sold a reproduction and with regard to being involved in a dodgy deal. Avoiding fraud takes time and time is money. Only deal with reputable sources, unless you are looking for a bargain at a garage sale.

The likelihood that you will be sold a fake or a forged item is a potential problem that you always face with investment collecting. There are generally ways of telling whether collectables are genuine and it is in your best interest to find out what they are.

Did you know ...

You are asking for trouble if you buy an allegedly genuine collectable for a fraction of the usual price. You can expect it to be a fake.

Basically you should take a commonsense approach when seeking to avoid fraud. Be realistic about the price of an item and be on guard if it seems artificially low. Seek to be as knowledgeable as the seller about any item you are interested in. If you are in doubt, either call in an expert or do not invest

Dealers

Dealers are in business to make a profit and therefore they have a financial interest in selling to you, but at the same time they are a wealth of information and they will happily share their knowledge if you make regular purchases from them. Get to know several of them.

Auctions

As a buyer, an auction may be the only opportunity you have to acquire a much-wanted item but do not expect to get a bargain. For a start, there will usually be a reserve on the item and, secondly, the prices in the catalogue may have been set at artificially low levels to attract people like you. As a seller, an auction may be the best opportunity to obtain the best price, but make sure you consider alternatives, such as selling on consignment through a dealer first. Auction houses have a vested interest in buyers and sellers going to auction, so treat their advice with scepticism. Whether you are buying or selling at auction, do your homework and note that some research costs money.

Patience

Patience is important when buying and selling collectables. A forced sale is never a good one, except by chance. When buying, you need to wait for good items to come onto the market. The types of purchases you make because you cannot live without an item are not the sort of investments that will make you money, so do not rush in, If you are on-selling an item, have regard to how, where and when you will resell it.

Timing

A 'buy and hold' strategy is usually appropriate with collectables because the longer you hold onto them the greater the increase in capital appreciation you can generally expect to earn. When speculating, you have to both buy and sell within a relatively short space of time. Effectively you have to aim to time the market, which is a difficult thing to do.

Restoration

As a general rule do not restore collectables that you wish to on-sell for a profit because a potential buyer will usually wish to do this themselves. You may be pleased with the restoration of your item but for a start the buyer may want a collectable in pristine condition. Investing in collectables is not like investing in property where paying money for renovations often has lucrative results.

Caveat emptor

In most cases caveat emptor—let the buyer beware—applies when investing in collectables. If a collectable is damaged or restored, it is up to the buyer to find this out beforehand. The difference in value between a collectable in original condition and one that is damaged can be alarming. For example, a stamp that is worth $200 in good condition is worth only $20 if some of the perforation teeth are missing.

Speculation

Although this book is not written for speculators, it should be mentioned that there are some basic prerequisites to being a successful speculator:

- You need to have a detached view.

- You have to know what to buy.

- You need to constantly monitor prices and markets—you cannot 'buy and forget' like a conventional investment collector can.

- You need to know when to sell.

- You must be prepared to pay income tax.

- You may have a lot of money tied up—speculation is not for the faint-hearted.

- You need to be an opportunist.

- You need to take advantage of arbitrage situations.

- You have to understand that quick gains can occur but so can quick losses.

Did you know … A speculator needs to be more flexible than a traditional investment collector because they may have to unexpectedly change their time frame from short term to medium or long term.

Making money out of art

If you have less than $5000 to invest in art, you are generally going to be limited to emerging artists. Works by emerging artists have the greatest scope for capital appreciation, but by the same token they may never take off. Only invest in them with funds earmarked for speculation. The first rule of thumb is: do not overcommit yourself to any one artist by buying just one artwork. The second rule is to obtain a certificate of authenticity. Then focus on emerging artists who have had exhibitions at galleries. The more reputable the gallery, the more confident you can be about a purchase.

When selecting a work by a mid-career artist choose an artist who is known to auction houses and galleries and who has won a prize or two, even if they are not well-known prizes. For example, some indigenous artists fit into this category. If you already own artwork by a mid-career artist, consider lending it to galleries free of charge. This will enhance provenance and provide publicity, which will increase its value.

Taxation

Do not forget to factor tax into your investment plan. Capital gains tax (CGT) is payable on collectables that cost more than $500 at your marginal rate of tax. You can claim a 50 per cent discount if you have held the collectable for longer than 12 months. Special provisions apply to deceased estates, and cars that cost $10 000 or less are exempt from CGT. Also you cannot claim capital losses from cars for CGT purposes. You will be liable to pay income tax if you are deemed to be in business.

Key points

- Focus on investing in collectables that interest you because you are more likely to become an expert investment collector.

- Focus on collectables that have liquid markets.

- Avoid collectables that have specific or impractical storage and maintenance requirements.

- Set a time frame for investing.

- Making money out of investing in collectables is like any other profit-making venture and you need an investment strategy.

- Diversify your investment portfolio and allocate a portion of your funds to collectables.

- There are sound arguments for diversification of your available funds within categories of collectables.

- You could incur losses as well as make profits, so do not invest more than you can afford to lose.

- Stick to mainstream collectables if you wish to make money because markets are established, more reliable and more liquid.

- Generally buy quality over quantity, but if you need an income stream, buy several lower value items and sell them off gradually.

- As a buyer it is mainly up to you to detect damage and repairs to items you purchase; caveat emptor — let the buyer beware.

- Special rules apply to speculating on collectables markets and it is not recommended for novice investors.

Useful resources

This section details the various sources of information that can assist you with investing in collectables. It is worth mentioning that sometimes 'collectables' is spelt 'collectibles', especially in the US, so search engines such as Google may use the words interchangeably.

Sources of information are vast and include books, journals, magazines, the internet, catalogues, radio and television programs, newspapers, exhibitions, newsletters, dealers, auction houses, professional valuers, clubs, and associations and societies.

Keep in mind that this section serves as an introduction only to where you might look for additional information. You will need to develop your own ideas and sources of information for your specific collectable interests. There are literally millions of possible sources of information regarding different collectables and it is easy to become overwhelmed by the sheer volume of information available. Ideally you should narrow this down by identifying four to six sources of information that are relevant to your particular interests. Once you do this it is advisable to check these regularly so that you remain up to date with developments in the market.

Auction houses

Auction houses are renowned for providing information, including features and dates of forthcoming auctions and catalogues, and price lists. Following are some auction houses you may come across:

- *Christies <www.christies.com>*
  Founded in 1766, Christies is one of the most famous auction houses in the world. Global auction sales of art alone in 2009 were around US$3.3 billion. Christies auctions items in over 80 categories, including art, antiques, wine, china, jewellery, photographs and collectables. It has 53 offices in 32 countries, including London, New York, Geneva, Milan, Hong Kong, Amsterdam, Melbourne and Sydney. Christies regularly makes sales at world record prices.

- *Sotheby's <www.sothebys.com>*
  Founded in 1744, Sotheby's is an auction house as famous as Christies. With over 100 offices worldwide, Sotheby's is larger than Christies. Like Christies, Sotheby's provides valuation and collection management services. If you are a small collector, it's worth noting that due to the size of these auction houses you might receive less attention than someone with a substantial collectable portfolio.

- *Freemans <www.freemansauction.com>*
  Auctioneers and valuers established in Philadelphia in 1805, this firm conducts more than 30 in-house auctions a year of American furniture, decorative and folk art, English and Continental furniture and decorative arts, Asian arts, fine American and European paintings, modern and contemporary art, rare books, fine prints, oriental rugs, fine jewellery and silver, and 20th- and 21st-century modern design objects.

- *Phillips de Pury and Company <www.phillipsdepury.com>*
  Originally established as Phillips in London in 1796. After a few name changes and changes in ownership it is now located in New York under the name of Phillips de Pury. The company focuses on the auction markets for contemporary art, design, jewellery, photography and first edition books.

- *Porro Art Consulting <www.porroartconsulting.it>*
  Formed in 2002 in Milan primarily as an art auction house.
  It has four main departments, namely Old Master paintings,
  19th-century paintings, modern and contemporary art, and
  decorative arts (glass, ceramics, furniture and works of art). Porro
  also provides collection management services for significant
  collections. You can request an English version of its website but
  some of the information, such as articles, is in Italian.

- *Doyle New York (DNY) <www.doylenewyork.com>*
  A well-known auctioneer and valuer of fine art, jewellery,
  furniture, decorations, coins, Asian works of art and a wide
  range of collectables. Doyle conducts about 40 auctions a year
  attracting buyers and sellers from around the world.

- *The Saleroom <www.the-saleroom.com>*
  Registered in London, the Saleroom conducts live auctions that
  are relayed via the internet for those interested in antiques, art
  and collectables. Real time audio and visual feeds enable you to be
  a part of the auction room experience as it is actually happening.
  The Saleroom was launched in 2006 and conducts its auctions in
  the UK, Europe, the US, Australia and Asia.

- *The Collector Network <www.collectornetwork.com>*
  Provides an online marketplace for more than 20 categories of
  collectables, including stamps, cars, coins, aircraft, militaria,
  music, rocks and minerals, paper money, toys, glass, clocks and
  watches, books, cards, cameras and photographs, autographs
  and so on. Its country of origin is unknown.

- *Bonhams <www.bonhams.com>*
  Established as an auction house in 1793 in London, after a
  few successful mergers Bonhams now has a network of offices
  and regional representatives in 25 countries. It has 19 regional
  offices in the UK and it also conducts sales in San Francisco, Los
  Angeles, New York, Sydney, France, Monaco, Hong Kong and
  Dubai. It specialises in art, antiquities, arms and armour, design
  prior to 1945, ceramics, clocks, glass, jewellery, Japanese art,
  collectables, miniatures and watches.

- *Lawsons <www.lawsons.com.au>*
  Lawsons and its sister company Lawson-Menzies are based in Sydney and Melbourne. James R Lawson established himself as a leading auctioneer in Sydney in the 1870s. In 2001 the Menzies Group of Companies acquired Lawsons' Sydney auction house. The auction house is well known in Australia for handling a wide range of property from domestic and general merchandise through to the upper end of the market for Australian and international art, antique furniture, fine wine, jewellery, decorative arts and prestigious house contents auctions.

- *Deutscher-Menzies <www.menziesartbrands.com>*
  Held its first auction in 1998. It focuses on art and needs to be differentiated from Lawson-Menzies previously mentioned.

- *Shapiro <www.shapiroauctioneers.com.au>*
  Shapiro's main saleroom is in Sydney, but it has offices in Melbourne, Adelaide, the Gold Coast and the Southern Highlands in NSW. The managing director, Andrew Shapiro, led a management buyout of Shapiro's predecessor, Phillips International Auctioneers, across Australia from Louis Vuitton Moet Hennessy in 2001. Shapiro is known for auctions of Australian and international art, Aboriginal art, 20th- and 21st-century design, traditional furniture and decorative art, in particular English and European silver and *objets d'vertu* (objects of virtue). Shapiro holds the Australian record price for a European painting and sculpture.

- *Leonard Joel <www.leonardjoel.com.au>*
  Founded in Melbourne in 1919, Leonard Joel has salerooms in South Yarra, Melbourne, and Double Bay, Sydney. Leonard Joel focuses on fine art, sculpture, jewellery, including watches, decorative arts, furniture, collectables, books and manuscripts, Asian art, period and contemporary prints and graphics, estates, single owner collections, and significant house contents auctions.

- *Mossgreen <www.mossgreen.com.au>*
  Focusing on single-owner collections covering fine art and antiques, Mossgreen has auction rooms in Melbourne and conducts on-site auctions or hires premises specifically to sell a collection. You can subscribe for up to 15 catalogues a year for $149.95.

Books on collectables

If you type 'antiques and collectables books' into Google, you will get more than 51 million results. Some websites are devoted to selling rare books rather than providing information about collectables, but even allowing for this, the number of books on collectables is daunting. One thing to watch out for is that while there is a huge range of second-hand collectables books on the market, most of them are out of date. This may not be important when assessing such things as the features of collectables and their rarity and condition, but it is important when it comes to current prices. One way of overcoming this is to go to the home page of a major Australian bookseller and insert 'antiques and collectables' into their search engine.

For example, if you enter 'collectables' into Dymocks' website <www.dymocks.com.au>, you will get 670 titles. However, more than half of these are unavailable. One of the titles you will see is *Millers Collectables Handbook 2010–2011* by Judith Miller and Mark Hill. Judith Miller is an authority on collectables, as is another well-known author of collectables books Alan Carter, and collectively they have published many books. Other titles in the Dymocks catalogue include such specialised subject areas as *The Collector's Encyclopedia of Buttons* by Sally C Luscombe. As a first step in your search for books about collectables it is a good idea to browse bookshops to see what is available, then check to see if what you are interested in can be purchased second-hand using an online website.

Online bookshops

We recommend the following online bookshops:

*   *Biblio <www.biblio.com>*
    An online bookshop formed in 2003 in North Carolina in the US. It provides a marketplace for bringing together buyers and sellers of books, whether they be individual sellers or bookshops. You can search for books by inputting a title or an author, including rare and out-of-print books. Note that international delivery charges can be expensive and might cost more than the cost of your book.

- *Abe Books <www.abebooks.com>*
  A larger and older version of the Biblio set-up, based in Canada. Thousands of booksellers user this website, which stocks around 140 million titles. There are special sections for signed books and rare and collectable books. As mentioned in the previous entry, beware that delivery charges may be more expensive than the cost of your book.

- *Amazon Books <www.amazon.com>*
  Another large online bookseller. If you type 'collectables' into its search engine, you will get over 14 200 results. First on the list is Judith Miller and Mark Hill's book *Millers Collectables Handbook 2010–2011*, which is available for less than half the recommended retail price. Again, however, delivery expenses can be high.

If you wish to focus on Australian online bookshops to minimise delivery charges, there are plenty available. If you insert 'online bookstore Australia' into Google, you will get more than 1.1 million results, including some overseas booksellers who cap delivery charges to Australia. You can refine your search by adding the word 'collectables', namely, 'online bookstore Australia collectables' and you will get more than 47 000 results, although this includes both booksellers selling rare and collectable books and those selling books about collectables.

Rare book dealers

Both Biblio and Abe Books sell rare and collectable books as do many other online booksellers. Dealers in rare and collectable books include:

- *Francis Edwards <www.francisedwards.co.uk>*
  An antiquarian bookseller established in London in 1855. It now has over 7000 antiquarian and second-hand books, with an emphasis on voyages and travel, naval and military, science and medicine, art and architecture, history, literature and the social sciences. Francis Edwards is a part of Hay Cinema Bookshop, which has about 200 000 books on all subjects.

- *Blackwell Rare Books <www.rarebooks.blackwell.co.uk>*
  A dealer in rare books founded in 1879 and based in Oxford in the UK. Benjamin Henry Blackwell was a founding member of the Antiquarian Booksellers' Association in 1906. The firm's

printed catalogues are sent overseas and sometimes advertise books it dealt with when it was first established.

- *Kestenbaum & Company* <www.kestenbaum.net>
  An auction house in New York that specialises in the sale of Western and oriental books, manuscripts and fine Judaica. It is the only auction house in the US that regularly focuses on Judaica, and it also conducts private treaty sales. Other services include valuations, cataloguing, advice on buying and selling at auction, and collection management consultation related to Hebraica and Judaica.

- *Pacific Book Auctions (PBA)* <www.pbagalleries.com>
  An auctioneer of fine books and private libraries based in San Francisco. PBA also sells on consignment and undertakes valuations.

- *Berkelouw Books* <www.berkelouw.com.au>
  Australia's largest rare and antiquarian, second-hand and new bookseller, with over two million books, many of which can be purchased online. The Berkelouw family began as booksellers in the Netherlands in 1812, and now have numerous stores in Sydney as well as stores in Melbourne and on the Sunshine Coast in Queensland. They provide a book binding and repair service as well. They also buy books and claim that they may be able to offer higher prices than can be achieved at auction.

Dealer associations

Some useful international dealer associations include:

- *The Art Dealers Association of America (ADAA)* <www.artdealers.org>
  Based in New York, the ADAA has 170 member galleries in more than 25 US cities. ADAA members deal primarily in paintings, sculptures, prints, drawings and photographs from the Renaissance to the present. Every ADAA member dealer has a home page on the ADAA website with a link to the dealer's own website. A dealer's own website contains detailed information about the art and artists represented by the dealer, what they have in stock and details of upcoming exhibitions. The ADAA seeks

to maintain high standards of ethical behaviour, cataloguing, professionalism, honesty and integrity, and membership is by invitation. The ADAA publishes a comprehensive 'Collector's Guide' to assist collectors when working with art dealers, which can be downloaded from its website.

- *The Society of London Art Dealers (SLAD)* <www.slad.org.uk>
  Based in London, SLAD was established in 1932 and has a current membership of about 100. It seeks to promote and protect the reputation of art dealers throughout the UK engaged in all forms of visual art. Membership is by invitation. SLAD's website lists member firms with links to their websites, which in turn show the artists they deal with and also often details of artwork they have in stock and upcoming exhibitions.

- *The American Philatelic Society (APS)* <www.stamps.org>
  Founded in 1886, the APS headquarters are located on the outskirts of State College in Pennsylvania. The APS is not a dealer association but rather it has nearly 44 000 members drawn from more than 110 countries and it is the largest non-profit society for stamp collectors in the world. The APS's objectives include promoting stamp collecting for everyone and assisting members to acquire and dispose of philatelic materials. It emphasises the mutual benefits that come from being a member and it regularly organises philatelic events.

- *The Contemporary Art Society (CAS)*
  <www.contemporaryartsociety.org>
  Another non-dealer association that might be useful. Based in London, CAS supports and develops public collections of contemporary art in the UK. The CAS aims to donate contemporary artworks to Member Museums and Galleries, but it is also a leading contemporary art consultancy provider in a diverse range of areas. Funds raised are used to support and develop further donations.

- *The Antwerp World Diamond Centre (AWDC)* <www.awdc.be>
  A body established by the diamond industry that represents the interests of the diamond business in Belgium, the centre of world diamond trading. Details of news and events and contact information can be found on its website.

- *The International Bank Note Society (IBNS)*
  <www.theibns.org>
  Formed in 1961, the IBNS objective is to 'promote, stimulate, and advance the study and knowledge of worldwide banknotes and paper currencies and all matters related thereto along educational, scientific and historical lines'.

- *The Professional Currency Dealer Association (PCDA)*
  <www.rarecurrency.net>
  Based in the US, the PCDA was founded in 1985 and it is comprised of more than 100 member specialists who deal in currency, stocks and bonds, fiscal documents and related paper items. One of its main goals is the promotion of ethical dealing between its members and the public. The PCDA hosts the National and World Paper Money Convention in St Louis each September.

- *The Antiquarian Booksellers Association (ABA)*
  <www.aba.org.uk>
  The main body for dealers in rare and fine books, manuscripts and allied materials in the UK and elsewhere. Founded in 1906, the ABA is based in London and it is the oldest association of its kind in the world. It runs a number of book fairs each year. Members are elected to the ABA on the basis of experience, expertise and integrity, and they are obliged to adhere to the ABA's Code of Good Practice.

- *The International League of Antiquarian Booksellers (ILAB)*
  <www.ilab.org>
  A federation of 22 national associations that represent rare book dealers worldwide. The ABA is one such association that represents the UK. Other associations are in Australia, Austria, Belgium, Brazil, Canada, China, Czech Republic, Denmark, Finland, France, Germany, Hungary, Italy, Japan, Republic of Korea, the Netherlands, Norway, Russian Federation, Spain, Sweden, Switzerland and the US. Links to country associations can be found on its website.

- *The Australian & New Zealand Association of Antiquarian Booksellers (ANZAAB)* <www.anzaab.com>
  Represents members of the antiquarian book business in Australia and New Zealand. ANZAAB was established in 1977 and it currently has 62 members. It regularly organises antiquarian book fairs in major cities. ANZAAB has a Code of Ethics that members are required to abide by. For example, ANZAAB particularly encourages high standards of accuracy in descriptions of items for sale.

- *The Coin Dealers Directory (CDD)* <www.numis.co.uk>
  Based in Blackpool in the UK. Its website contains information on coin dealers in the UK and Northern Ireland on a regional basis. By clicking on one of the regions listed on the CDD's website you can see a range of coin dealers.

- *Federation of European Professional Numismatic Associations (FENAP)* <www.numis.co.uk/fenap.html)>
  The CDD provides a link to FENAP. It is comprised of associations that aim to work together towards a common system of value added tax on coins within the European Community. FENAP members also provide each other with details of counterfeit and stolen coins and liaise on such matters as auction and fair dates. There are member associations in Austria, Belgium, Denmark, France, Germany, Italy, Luxembourg, the Netherlands, the Republic of Northern Ireland, Spain, Sweden and the UK. Switzerland is an associate member. FENAP does not have its own website and address and fax details of member associations are given on the CDD website.

- *The British Numismatic Trade Association (BNTA)* <www.bnta.net>
  Based in London, the BNTA is the British member of FENAP. It was founded in 1973 and represents the interests of more than 60 firms. The BNTA's Membership Directory lists members by county and in alphabetical order, and it identifies whether a dealer has retail premises. Brief details of a dealer's specialities are also provided to help collectors locate dealers who can assist them. The BNTA believes that within its membership there are dealers who can help a collector on virtually any topic, although the BNTA itself does not give advice. Applicants for membership must be

sponsored by two existing members and they need to agree to abide by the association's Code of Ethics, which is published on its website. Around September each year the BNTA organises Coinex, which is the most significant international coin fare in the UK.

- *The Ancient Coin Collectors Guild (ACCG)* <www.accg.us>
  Based in Montana in the US, the ACCG seeks to preserve the interests of those who collect ancient coins. It is not a dealer association but rather seeks primarily to preserve the right of collectors to own ancient coins irrespective of the wishes of the governments of the countries from where the coins originated.

- *The American Numismatic Society (ANS)* <www.numismatics.org>
  Based in New York, the ANS is focused on the study of coins, currency, medals, tokens and related items from all cultures. It was founded in 1858 and it has the foremost research collection and library dedicated to numismatics in the US. Its resources are used to support research and education in numismatics for the benefit of academics, collectors, professional numismatists and the general public. At last count the ANS had 1875 individual Associates (112 institutional), 198 individual Fellows and Honorary Fellows, and 54 individual Corresponding Members (foreign).

- *The Association of International Photography Art Dealers (AIPAD)* <www.aipad.com>
  Based in New York, AIPAD has members in the US, Canada, Australia, Europe and Japan. It represents dealers from more than 70 galleries and members are required to abide by a Code of Ethics. It has a show in New York each year.

- *International Auctioneers (IA)* <www.interntaionalauctioneers.com>
  An association of eight artwork auction houses with its headquarters in Geneva, Switzerland. IA can assist you to find lots in hundreds of auction catalogues accounting for half-a-million artworks offered each year. The auction houses comprising IA are Artcurial in Paris; Bukowskis in Stockholm and Helsinki; Bruun Rasmussen in Copenhagen and Aarhus (Denmark); Dorotheum in Vienna and Prague; Porro & C. in Milan; Koller Auctions Ltd in Zurich and Geneva; Lempertz in Cologne; and Swann Auction Galleries in New York.

- *The Australasian Numismatic Dealer's Association (ANDA)*
  <www.anda.com.au>
  Established in Victoria in 1995, ANDA aims to promote,
  develop and maintain a high standard of business ethics among
  numisamists and philatelists and those engaged in merchandising
  collectables.

Numismatists

Numismatists predominantly deal in coins and related items, such as
banknotes and medals, but some may also deal in stamps.

- *Stacks Numismatics <www.stacks.com>*
  Primarily an auction house for rare coins based in New York.
  Established in 1935, it conducts valuations and has a retail
  department.

- *Spinks <www.spink.com>*
  Primarily an auction house for rare coins based in London. It was
  founded in 1666 and it is world renowned. Spinks undertakes
  valuations and conducts retail sales as well.

- *Dix Noonan Webb (DNW) <www.dnw.co.uk>*
  An auction house and valuer based in London. It deals in British
  and world coins, ancient coins, Celtic coins, tokens, tickets and
  passes, historic and art medals, banknotes, numismatic books, war
  medals, orders and decorations, militaria and military books.

- *Baldwin's <www.baldwin.co.uk>*
  Established in London in 1872. It is a dealer and auctioneer of
  coins, medals, tokens, banknotes and numismatic books, and
  offers free verbal valuations. Check its website for information on
  how to obtain a valuation.

- *Coincraft <www.coincraft.com>*
  Established in London in 1955, Coincraft emphasises that it
  deals with collectors only rather than selling coins as investments.
  However, it buys and sells coins from dealers and the public, so it
  can still be of interest to collectors. It deals in coins, banknotes,
  ancient coins, medallions and antiquities.

- *Nomos AG <www.nomosag.com>*
  Founded in 1972 in Luzern, Switzerland, Nomas AG specialises in rare and beautiful ancient, medieval and early modern coins and medals presented for auction or private treaty sale. It has both institutional and private clients and provides advice.

- *Collect Paper Money (CPM) <www.collectpapermoney>*
  An online store for banknotes. CPM's website says that it focuses on beginning and intermediate collectors. Its country of origin is unknown. Its website contains tips and information for collecting banknotes and special offers.

- *Morton and Eden <www.mortonandeden.com>*
  Specialist auctioneers of rare coins, war medals, orders and decorations, historical medals and banknotes. Many of its staff are former members of the Coins and Medals Department at Sotheby's. It provides valuations and conducts private treaty sales.

- *The Rare Coin Company (RCC) <www.rarecoin.com.au>*
  Established over 25 years ago, RCC buys and sells rare Australian coins and banknotes and selected rare world coins and banknotes. It has its main office in Albany, Western Australia, but it has open days in major cities. It provides a free valuation service for portfolios valued at over $5000 and it offers insured storage facilities for a fee. It will also sell coins and banknotes on consignment or repurchase them at a negotiated price (and at its discretion). The RCC makes many sales online accompanied by its guarantee of authenticity.

- *The Perth Mint <www.perthmint.com.au>*
  Probably best known for producing and storing gold bullion, the Perth Mint also manufactures 99.99 per cent gold and silver coins for sale to the public. Smaller coins have limited mintages, which makes them attractive to investment collectors. You can subscribe to its free newsletter; check its website for details.

- *Noble Numismatics <www.noble.com.au>*
  Established in Sydney as Spink & Son (Australia) in 1976, its Melbourne office was opened in 1982. In its present form, Nobles was incorporated in 1993. It trades in coins, medals, stamps, banknotes and related material. Since its inception, the company

has conducted more than 90 major public auctions realising in excess of $220 million. It also has a retail trade and it has handled many of Australia's most important collections and deceased estates.

Stamps

Many numismatists also deal in stamps and note that some stamp dealers also deal in other items unrelated to philately.

- *Stanley Gibbons <www.stanleygibbons.com>*
  A listed company in the UK, whose principal activities are dealing in stamps, autographs, rare records and related memorabilia, the development and operation of collectable websites, philatelic publishing, auctioneering, mail order, retailing and the manufacture of philatelic accessories. Basically Stanley Gibbons is one of the foremost stamp dealers in the world.

- *Brandon Stamps <www.brandonstamps.com>*
  A rare stamp dealer established in London in 1962. It stocks a large range of rare stamps with an emphasis on British themes, and it provides investment advice.

- *The Australasian Philatelic Traders' Association (APTA) <www.apta.com.au>*
  Established for over 60 years, the APTA provides useful information on stamp collecting, including details of forthcoming auctions, events, shows and fairs, and it publishes an annual Dealer Directory. Members must abide by a Code of Ethics.

Art galleries

There are major art galleries in all states and territories throughout Australia. There are also smaller galleries in cities and towns that hold exhibitions. It usually does not cost anything to browse an art gallery, although for more important exhibitions you may be charged an admission fee. If you enter 'art galleries' into Google, you will get over 72 million results. Major listings include:

- *The National Gallery of Australia (NGA), Canberra*
  <www.nga.gov.au>
  The NGA holds exhibitions that attract people from all over Australia. It publishes a free fortnightly email newsletter, 'Artonline', about upcoming events, exhibitions and special offers.

- *The National Gallery of Victoria (NGV), Melbourne*
  <www.ngv.vic.gov.au>
  The oldest public art museum in Australia, having been established in 1861. Check its website for information on NGA's numerous programs, reports and policies.

- *The Art Gallery of NSW (AGNSW), Sydney*
  <www.artgallery.nsw.gov.au>
  Visited by over 1.3 million people each year. The AGNSW was established in 1874 and it is the home of the highly publicised Archibald Prize exhibition.

- *The Art Gallery of Western Australia (AGWA), Perth*
  <www.artgallery.wa.gov.au>
  The AGWA was established in 1895 and houses the State Art Collection, which includes one of the world's best collections of Indigenous art.

- *The Art Gallery of South Australia (AGSA), Adelaide*
  <www.artgallery.sa.gov.au>
  The AGSA has numerous collections and exhibitions.

- *Museums and Art Galleries of the Northern Territory (MAGNT), Darwin* <www.magnt.nt.gov.au>
  A prominent event established in 1984 is the Telstra National Aboriginal & Torres Strait Islander Art Award (NATSIAA), which is known for attracting diverse and innovative Indigenous art. It is held yearly at MAGNT and comprises about 100 preselected artworks.

- *The Queensland Art Gallery (QAG)/Gallery of Modern Art, Brisbane*
  <www.qag.gov.au>
  Established in 1895 as the Queensland National Art Gallery. The Gallery of Modern Art opened in December 2006 and it complements the QAG.

- *The Tasmanian Museum and Art Gallery (TMAG), Hobart*
  <www.tmag.tas.gov.au>
  Features exhibitions and research facilities.

- *The Museum of Contemporary Art (MCA), Sydney*
  <www.mca.com.au>
  Provides free exhibitions of contemporary art. You can also sign
  up for a free email newsletter that gives information on the latest
  exhibitions and events.

Online art resources

There are numerous online resources you can use when researching art,
including details such as a history of auction prices.

- *The Australian Art Sales Digest (AASD)* <www.aasd.com.au>
  Comprises a database of over 420 000 works of art by more than
  40 000 artists. It contains art market information for Australia
  and New Zealand as well as auction results from 1969 to the
  present. Subscription rates are $30 for one month or $255 for
  a year.

- *The Art Record* <www.artrecord.com>
  Similar to AASD, the Art Record provides auction results for
  Australian and New Zealand Art since the early 1970s. The cost
  of subscribing is $9 for one week, $30 for one month or $155 for
  a year.

- *Artnet* <www.artnet.com>
  Listed on the Frankfurt Stock Exchange but operates a subsidiary
  in the US. Artnet is an online gallery and online auction house
  that has a database of auction prices going back to 1985 that
  covers 500 auction houses accounting for more than four million
  results and over 188 000 artists. Cost of access is US$29.95
  per month for up to 30 searches or US$500 a year for up to
  185 searches.

- *Beautiful Asset Advisors* <www.artasanasset.com>
  A US website that views graphs of the Mei Moses Art Index,
  which enables the user to assess the returns from investing in art

compared with other assets. You can also view market adjusted returns for individual artists. Yearly rates for a Silver subscription costs US$100, while a Gold subscription costs US$250.

Art fairs

Art fairs are held over a period of days, or even a week, in overseas cities and attending them can be combined with a holiday. Art fairs only exist in Australia on a very limited scale.

- *Art Basel <www.artbasel.com>*
  The premier international art show for modern and contemporary work, Art Basel is held in the early part of the European summer in Basel, Switzerland, which is on the Rhine at the intersection of Switzerland, France and Germany. It features more than 2500 artists from around 300 galleries from North America, Latin America, Europe, Asia and Africa, and exhibits include examples of the great masters of modern art and of emerging artists. Over 60 000 people attend each year and you can sign up to the show's mailing list on its website.

- *Art Basel Miami Beach <www.artbaselmiamibeach.com>*
  Affiliated with Art Basel, this is the most significant art show in the US. It features a selection of over 2000 20th- and 21st-century artworks from more than 250 galleries, and it is billed as the favourite winter meeting place for the international art world. It is attended by collectors, artists, dealers, curators, critics and art enthusiasts.

- *Art Dubai <www.artdubai.ae>*
  A show comprised of over 70 galleries from more than 30 countries from the Middle East and South Asia. The show is for collectors, artists and art professionals.

- *Art Fair Tokyo <www.artfairtokyo.com>*
  Held each year in April, Art Fair Tokyo comprises more than 130 international and domestic galleries with over 40 000 visitors. It covers a wide variety of genres, including modern and contemporary art and antiques.

- *The European Fine Art Fair* <www.tefaf.com>
  Held in Maastricht in the Netherlands, this art fair comprises over 250 art and antique dealers from more than 15 countries.

- *The Hong Kong International Art Fair* <www.hongkongartfair.com>
  Held in May each year. The fair is comprised of over 150 galleries from more than 25 countries and the number of attendees exceeds 45 000.

Art rental dealers

Dealers who can advise you on suitable artwork to buy if you wish to rent it out and derive an income stream include:

- Art Equity Pty Ltd <www.artequity.com.au>, telephone (02) 9262 6660

- Artbank <www.artbank.gov.au>, telephone 1800 251 651

- Smith & Hall <www.smithandhall.com.au>, telephone (02) 8823 4300.

Artbank is a government-funded initiative that specialises in contemporary art. It has showrooms in Melbourne, Sydney and Perth. Art Equity and Smith & Hall have galleries in Sydney.

As mentioned in previous chapters, art rental dealers guarantee returns of 5 per cent to 8 per cent before tax over two to three years net of potential capital appreciation. Of course such a guarantee is only as good as the organisation that gives it. Keep in mind also that the value of an artwork may depreciate instead of appreciate during the time it is rented out.

Media

The media is a useful resource for finding out about collectables. There are sometimes regular features in newspapers and magazines, as well as on television or on radio. Publications such as magazines and newspapers occasionally contain articles on art and other collectables. You will have to track them down, though, so let others know you are an investment collector and encourage them to keep an eye out for you. Following are some media sources worth looking out for.

Television programs

Mention has already been made of the Nine Network's *Antiques Roadshow* (<www.pbs.org/wgbh/antiquesuk/>) and the ABC's *Collectors* (<www. abc.net.au/tv/collectors/>) in previous chapters. *Antiques Roadshow* is produced for PBS by the BBC in association with WGBH Boston and it sometimes comes to Australia. *Collectors* invites audience interaction via its website, including an opportunity to guess what a weekly mystery object is.

Radio programs

Some radio programs offer listeners the opportunity to call the station and ask an experienced valuer about the worth of their collectables. In Sydney, Radio 2UE is one network that does this. Be aware that the valuers are giving opinions off the top of their head without doing any research and may well be wide of the mark. Valuations given are generally less than $200, so do not expect to obtain an opinion about an expensive artwork, for example.

Newspapers

Articles on collectables, especially where fraud is involved, often appear in newspapers. Some newspapers also have regular features on collectables. For example, the *Sydney Morning Herald* usually publishes a column on Wednesday in its Money section. The *Australian Financial Review* often publishes articles on collectables with an investment orientation. Do not overlook the fact that international newspapers also contain articles on collectables. For example, the *Wall Street Journal* often provides useful financial information with an international flavour.

Magazines

The most useful magazine articles from an investment viewpoint are those that appear in such magazines as *SmartInvestor*. However, there are magazines that focus solely on collectables. The *Collectors* television program has a companion magazine also called *Collectors,* which is published irregularly. It contains many articles on collectables, including values, and is worth buying. *Australian Art Collector* is published quarterly and is billed as Australia's art market magazine. In the past it has included a series of features such as what to buy under $3000 or the 50 most collectable Australian artists, but at around $20 a copy the magazine is not cheap. Check its website <www.artcollector.net.au> for subscription details.

Art Asia Pacific magazine is published bi-monthly and costs US$72 per year for a subscription, including postage. For further information, including extracts, go to <www.artasiapacific.com>. The *Art Market Report* <www.aamr.com.au> is also published bi-monthly and is read by art collectors, artists, auctioneers, gallery owners, curators and investors. It costs $40 per year for an online subscription or $90 if posted.

Art Almanac was established in 1974 and provides information on Australia's art galleries, exhibitions, artists, art events, auctions, art prizes, art schools and related art services. It is published 11 times a year and costs $40 including GST. Visit <ww.art-almanac.com.au>.

Other magazines are published on specific types of collectables, although you should always investigate the availability of free newsletters first.

Index

Printed in Australia
13 Mar 2017
624217